"Father sat at the table with the fat family Bible open at the page on which the names of his seven other children were written. He added ours, Richard and Emily, which as well as being ours were his own name and Mother's. The covers of the Bible banged, shutting us all in. The Bible says that I was born on the thirteenth day of December, 1871."

Emily Carr, *Growing Pains*

"The art of Emily Carr is exactly the same in her writing as in her pictures. It is the art of eliminating all but the essentials — the essentials for her, that is, the elements which contribute to her impression — and then setting these down in the starkest, most compressed form. She had no wish to paint, or to describe in words, the things around her as other people saw them; the camera and the phonograph could do that: it was not work for the artist. What she wanted was to study the things and the events which she felt contained material, until she had extracted that material and thrown everything else away."

B. K. Sandwell in *Saturday Night*

THE BOOK OF SMALL

THE BOOK OF SMALL

EMILY CARR

CLARKE, IRWIN & COMPANY LIMITED

Toronto, Vancouver

Copyright, 1942
Clarke, Irwin & Company Limited

First educational edition, 1951
(in two volumes: *The Book of
Small* and *A Little Town and a Little Girl*)

First paperback edition, 1966

ISBN 0-7720-0223-1

5 6 7 8 JD 77 76 75 74

Printed in Canada

TO IRA DILWORTH

CONTENTS

THE BOOK OF SMALL

Sunday

ALL OUR Sundays were exactly alike. They began on Saturday night after Bong the Chinaboy had washed up and gone away, after our toys, dolls and books, all but *The Peep of Day* and Bunyan's *Pilgrim's Progress,* had been stored away in drawers and boxes till Monday, and every Bible and prayer-book in the house was puffing itself out, looking more important every minute.

Then the clothes-horse came galloping into the kitchen and straddled round the stove inviting our clean clothes to mount and be aired. The enormous wooden tub that looked half coffin and half baby-bath was set in the middle of the kitchen floor with a rag mat for dripping on laid close beside it. The great iron soup pot, the copper wash-boiler and several kettles covered the top of the stove, and big sister Dede filled them by working the kitchen pump-handle furiously. It was a sad old pump and always groaned several times before it poured. Dede got the brown windsor soap, heated the towels and put on a thick white apron with a bib. Mother unbuttoned us and by that time the pots and kettles were steaming.

Dede scrubbed hard. If you wriggled, the flat of the long-handled tin dipper came down spankety on your skin.

As soon as each child was bathed Dede took it pick-a-back and rushed it upstairs through the cold house. We were allowed to say our prayers kneeling in bed on Saturday night, steamy, brown-windsory prayers—then we cuddled down and tumbled very comfortably into Sunday.

At seven o'clock Father stood beside our bed and said, "Rise up! Rise up! It's Sunday, children." He need not have told us; we knew Father's Sunday smell—Wright's coal-tar soap and camphor. Father had a splendid chest of camphor-wood which had come from England round the Horn in a sailing-ship with him. His clean clothes lived in it and on Sunday he was very camphory. The chest was high and very heavy. It had brass handles and wooden knobs. The top let down as a writing desk with pigeon-holes; below there were little drawers for handkerchiefs and collars and long drawers for clothes. On top of the chest stood Father's locked desk for papers. The key of it was on his ring with lots of others. This desk had a secret drawer and a brass plate with R. H. CARR engraved on it.

On top of the top desk stood the little Dutchman, a china figure with a head that took off and a stomach full of little candies like coloured hailstones. If we had been very good all week we got hailstones Sunday morning.

Family prayers were uppish with big words on Sunday—reverend awe-ful words that only God and Father understood.

No work was done in the Carr house on Sunday. Everything had been polished frightfully on Saturday and all Sunday's food cooked too. On Sunday morning Bong milked the cow and went away from breakfast until evening milking-time. Beds were made, the dinner-table set, and then we got into our very starchiest and most uncomfortable clothes for church.

Our family had a big gap in the middle of it where William, John and Thomas had all been born and died in quick succession, which left a wide space between Dede and Tallie and the four younger children.

Lizzie, Alice and I were always dressed exactly alike. Father wanted my two big sisters to dress the same, but they rebelled, and Mother stood behind them. Father thought we looked like orphans if we were clothed differently. The Orphans sat in front of us at church. No two of them had anything alike. People gave them all the things their own children had grown out of—some of them were very strange in shape and colour.

When we were all dressed, we went to Mother's room to be looked over. Mother was very delicate and could not get up early or walk the two miles to church, and neither could Tallie or little Dick.

Father went to Dr. Reid's Presbyterian Church at the corner of Pandora and Blanshard streets. Father was not particularly Presbyterian, but he was a little deaf and he liked Dr. Reid because, if we sat at the top of the church, he could hear his sermons. There was just the Orphans in front of us, and the stove in front of them. The heat of the stove sent them all to sleep. But Dr. Reid was a kind preacher—he did not bang the Bible, nor shout to wake them up. Sometimes I went to sleep too, but I tried not to because of what happened at home after Sunday's dinner.

If the road had not been so crooked it would have been a straight line from the gate of our lily-field to the church door. We did not have to turn a single corner. Lizzie, Alice and I walked in the middle of the road and took hands. Dede was on one end of us and Father on the other. Dede carried a parasol, and Father, a fat yellow stick, not a flourish stick but one to walk with. If we met anything, we dangled in a row behind Father like the tail of a kite.

We were always very early for church and could watch the Orphans march in. The Matron arranged every bad Orphan between two good ones, and put very little ones beside big ones, then she set herself down behind them where she could watch and poke any Orphan that needed it. She was glad when the stove sent them all to sleep and did not poke unless an Orphan had adenoids and snored.

The minute the church bell stopped a little door in front of the Orphans opened, and Dr. Reid came out and somebody behind him shut the door, which was rounded at the top and had a reverend shut.

Dr. Reid had very shiny eyes and very red lips. He wore a black gown with two little white tabs like the tail of a bird sticking out from under his beard. He carried a roll in his hand like Moses, and on it were all the things that he was going to say to us. He walked slowly between the Orphans and the stove and climbed into the pulpit and prayed. The S's sizzled in his mouth as if they were frying. He was a very nice minister and the only parson that Father ever asked to dinner.

The moment Dr. Reid amened, we rushed straight out of the church off home. Father said it was very bad taste for people to stand gabbing at church doors. We came down Church Hill, past the Convent Garden, up Marvin's Hill, through the wild part of Beacon Hill Park into our own gate. The only time we stopped was to gather some catnip to take home to the cats, and the only turn we made was into our own gate.

Our Sunday dinner was cold saddle of mutton. It was roasted on Saturday in a big tin oven on legs, which was pushed up to the open grate fire in the breakfast-room. Father had this fire-place specially built just like the ones in England. The oven fitted right up to it. He thought everything English was much better than anything Canadian. The oven came round the Horn with him, and the big pewter hot-water dishes that he ate his chops and steaks off, and the heavy mahogany furniture and lots of other things that you could not buy in Canada then. The tin oven had a jack which you wound up like a clock and it turned the roast on a spit. It said 'tick, tick, tick' and turned the meat one way, and then 'tock, tock, tock' and turned it the other. The meat sizzled and sputtered. Someone was always opening the little tin door in the back to baste it, using a long iron spoon, with the dripping that was caught in a pan beneath the meat. Father said no roast under twenty pounds was worth eating because the juice had all run out of it, so it was lucky he had a big family.

Red currant jelly was served with the cold mutton, and potato salad and pickled cabbage, afterwards there was deep apple pie with lots of Devonshire cream. In the centre of the dinner-table, just below the cruet stand, stood an enormous loaf of bread. Mr. Harding, the baker, cooked one for Father every Saturday. It was four loaves baked in one so that it did not get as stale as four small loaves would have. It was made cottage-loaf-shape—two storeys high with a dimple in the top.

When dinner was finished, Father folded his napkin very straight, he even slipped his long fingers inside each fold again after it was in the ring, for Father always wanted everything straight and right. Then he looked up one side of the table and down the other. We all tried not to squirm because he always picked the squirmiest. When he had decided who should start, he said, "Tell me what you remember of the sermon."

If Dede was asked first, she "here and there'd" all over the sermon. If it was Lizzie, she plowed steadily through from text to amen. Alice always remembered the text. Sometimes I remembered one of Dr. Reid's jokes, that is if I was asked first—if not I usually said, "The others have told it all, Father," and was dreadfully uncomfortable when Father said, "Very well; repeat it, then."

When we had done everything we could with Dr. Reid's sermon, Father went into the sitting room to take his Sunday nap, Mother read, and Dede took hold of our religion.

She taught Sunday School in Bishop Cridge's house, to a huge family of Balls and an enormous family of Fawcetts, a smarty boy called Eddy, a few other children who came and went, and us. The Bishop's invalid sister sat in the room all the time. Her cheeks were hollow, she had sharp eyes with red rims, sat by the fire, wore a cap and coughed, not because she had to, but just to remind us that she was watching and listening.

From dinner till it was time to go to the Bishop's, we learned collects, texts and hymns. Dede was shamed because the Balls, the Fawcetts and all the others did better than I who was her own sister.

You got a little text-card when you knew your lessons. When you had six little cards you had earned a big text-card. I hardly ever got a little card and always lost it on the way home, so that I never earned a big one. I could sing much better than Addie Ball, who just talked the hymns out very loud, but Dede only told me not to shout and let Addie groan away without any tune at all.

When Dede marched us home, Father was ready, and Mother had her hat on, to start for the Sunday walk around our place. Dede stayed home to get the tea, but first she played very loud hymns on the piano. They followed us all round the fields. Tallie was not strong enough for the walking so she lay on the horse-hair sofa in the drawing-room looking very pretty, resting up for her evening visitor. Lizzie squeezed out of coming whenever she could because she had rather creep into a corner and learn more texts. She had millions of texts piled up inside her head just waiting for things to happen, then she pushed the right text over onto them. If you got mad any time after noon, the sun was going to set on your wrath. You could feel the great globe getting hotter and hotter and making your mad fiercer because of the way the text stirred it up. If you did not see things just in Lizzie's way, you were dead in your sins.

So the rest of us started for the Sunday walk. We went out the side door into the garden, through ever so many gates and the cow-yard, on into a shrubbery which ran round two sides of the cow pasture, but was railed off to keep the cows from destroying the shrubs. A twisty little path ran through the shrubbery. Father wanted his place to look exactly like England. He planted cowslips and primroses and hawthorn hedges and all the Englishy flowers. He had stiles and meadows and took away all the wild Canadian-ness and made it as meek and English as he could.

We did not take the twisty path but a straight little one of red earth, close up under the hedge. We went singly, Father first, then Mother with little Dick by the hand. Because of William, John and Thomas being dead, Mother's only boy was Dick. He had a lovely little face with blue eyes and yellow curls. He wore a little pant suit with a pleated skirt over the pants which came half-way down over his thin little legs. These suits were very fashionable for small boys—Mr. Wilson knew that they would sell, because of the jack-knife on a knotted cord brought through the buttonhole and dropping into a pocket on the chest. When boys saw these knife suits they teased and teased till they got one. Alice plodded along behind Dick, her arms hung loose and floppy. Father thought all make-believes were wicked on Sunday, even make-believe babies, so her darling dolls sat staring on the shelf in our bedroom all day. I came last and wished that our Sunday walk was not quite so much fenced. First there was the thorny hedge and then the high pickets.

Mr. Green, my friend Edna's father, took his family to the beach every Sunday. They clattered and chattered past our place having such jokes. I poked my head through the hedge to whisper,

"Hello, Edna!"

"Hello! How dull you do look walking round your own cow-field! Come to the beach with us."

"I don't think I can."

"Ask your mother."

I scraped between Alice and the hedge.

"Can I, Mother?"

"Your Father likes you to walk with him on Sunday."

I stuck my head through the thorns again, and shook it. Once I actually asked Father myself if I could go with the Greens, and he looked as hurt as if I'd hit him.

"Are my nine acres not enough, but you must want to tear over the whole earth? Is the Sabbath a right day to go pleasuring on the beach?" he said.

But one Sunday I did go with the Greens. Father had the gout and did not know. We had fun and I got "show-off" from being too happy. The boys dared me to walk a log over the sea, and I fell in. When I came home dripping, Lizzie had a text about my sin finding me out.

But I was telling about the family taggling along the path

under the hedge. Father's stick was on the constant poke, pushing a root down or a branch up, or a stone into place, for he was very particular about everything being just right.

As we neared the top corner of our big field, that one wild place where the trees and bushes were allowed to grow thick and tangled, and where there was a deep ditch with stinging-nettles about it, and a rank, muddy smell, Father began to frown and to walk faster and faster till we were crouched down in the path, running after one another like frightened quail. If there were voices on the other side of the hedge, we raced like mad.

This corner of Father's property always made him very sore. When he came from England he bought ten acres of fine land adjoining Beacon Hill Park, which was owned by the City of Victoria. It took Father a lot of money to clear his land. He left every fine tree he could, because he loved trees, but he cleared away the scrub to make meadows for the cows, and a beautiful garden. Then he built what was considered in 1863 a big fine house. It was all made of California redwood. The chimneys were of California brick and the mantelpieces of black marble. Every material used in the building of Father's house was the very best, because he never bought anything cheap or shoddy. He had to send far away for most of it, and all the time his family was getting bigger and more expensive, too; so, when a Mrs. Lush came and asked if he would sell her the corner acre next to the Park and farthest away from our house, and as she offered a good price, he sold. But first he said, "Promise me that you will never build a Public House on the land," and Mrs. Lush said, "No, Mr. Carr, I never will." But as soon as the land was hers, Mrs. Lush broke her word, and put up one of the horridest saloons in Victoria right there. Father felt dreadful, but he could not do anything about it, except to put up a high fence and coax that part of the hawthorn hedge to grow as tall and be as prickly as it could.

Mrs. Lush's Public House was called the Park Hotel, but afterwards the name was changed to the Colonist Hotel. It was just a nice drive from Esquimalt, which was then a

Naval Station, and hacks filled with tipsy sailors and noisy ladies drove past our house going to the Park Hotel in the daytime and at night. It hurt Father right up till he was seventy years old, when he died.

After we had passed the Park Hotel acre we went slow again so that Father could enjoy his land. We came to the "pickets", a sort of gate without hinges; we lifted the pickets out of notches in the fence and made a hole through which we passed into the lily field.

Nothing, not even fairyland, could have been so lovely as our lily field. The wild lilies blossomed in April or May but they seemed to be always in the field, because, the very first time you saw them, they did something to the back of your eyes which kept themselves there, and something to your nose, so that you smelled them whenever you thought of them. The field was roofed by tall, thin pine trees. The ground underneath was clear and grassed. The lilies were thickly sprinkled everywhere. They were white, with gold in their hearts and brown eyes that stared back into the earth because their necks hooked down. But each lily had five sharp white petals rolling back and pointing to the tree-tops, like millions and millions of tiny quivering fingers. The smell was fresh and earthy. In all your thinkings you could picture nothing more beautiful than our lily field.

We turned back towards our house then, and climbed a stile over a snake fence. On the other side of the fence was a mass of rock, rich and soft with moss, and all round it were mock orange and spirea and oak trees.

Father and Mother sat down upon the rock. You could see the thinking in their eyes. Father's was proud thinking as he looked across the beautiful place that he had made out of wild Canadian land—he thought how splendidly English he had made it look. Mother's eyes followed our whispered Sunday playing.

When Father got up, Mother got up too. We walked round the lower hay field, going back into the garden by the back gate, on the opposite side of the house from which we had left. Then we admired the vegetables, fruit and flowers until the front door flew open and Dede jangled the big brass dinner bell for us to come in to tea.

When the meal was finished the most sober part of all Sunday came, and that was the Bible reading. Church and Sunday School had partly belonged to Dr. Reid and Dede. The Bible reading was all God's. We all came into the sitting-room with our faces very straight and our Bibles in our hands.

There was always a nice fire in the grate, because, even in summer, Victoria nights are chilly. The curtains were drawn across the windows and the table was in front of the fire. It was a round table with a red cloth, and the brass lamp sitting in the middle threw a fine light on all the Bibles when we drew our chairs in close.

Father's chair was big and stuffed, Mother's low, with a high back. They faced each other where the table began to turn away from the fire. Between their chairs where it was too hot for anyone to sit, the cats lay sprawling on the rug before the fire. We circled between Father and Mother on the other side of the table.

Father opened the big Family Bible at the place marked by the cross-stitch text Lizzie had worked. In the middle of the Bible, between the "old" and the "new", were some blank pages, and all of us were written there. Sometimes Father let us look at ourselves and at William, John and Thomas who were each written there twice, once for being born, and once for dying. That was the only time that John, Thomas and William seemed to be real and take part in the family's doings. We did little sums with their Bible dates, but could never remember if they had lived for days or years. As they were dead before we were born, and we had never known them as Johnny- or Tommy- or Willie-babies, they felt old and grown up to us.

Tallie was more interested in the marriage page. There was only one entry on it, "Richard and Emily Carr", who were Father and Mother.

Tallie said, "Father, Mother was only eighteen when she married you, wasn't she?"

"Yes," said Father, "and had more sense than some girls I could name at twenty." He was always very frowny when the doorbell rang in the middle of Bible reading and Tallie went out and did not come back.

We read right straight through the Bible, begat chapters and all, though even Father stuck at some of the names.

On and on we read till the nine o'clock gun went off at Esquimalt. Father, Mother, and Dede set their watches by the gun and then we went on reading again until we came to the end of the chapter. The three smallest of us had to spell out most of the words and be told how to say them. We got most dreadfully sleepy. No matter how hard you pressed your finger down on the eighth verse from the last one you had read, when the child next to you was finishing and kicked your shin you jumped and the place was lost. Then you got scolded and were furious with your finger. Mother said, "Richard, the children are tired," but Father said, "Attention! Children" and went right on to the end of the chapter. He thought it was rude to God to stop in a chapter's middle nor must we shut our Bibles up with a glad bang when at last we were through.

No matter how sleepy we had been during Bible reading, when Father got out the *Sunday at Home* we were wide awake to hear the short chapter of the serial story. Father did not believe in fairy stories for children. *At the Back of the North Wind* was as fairy as anything, but, because it was in the *Sunday at Home,* Father thought it was all right.

We kissed Mother good night. While the others were kissing Father I ran behind him (I did so hate kissing beards) and, if Father was leaning back, I could just reach his bald spot and slap the kiss there.

Dede lighted the candle and we followed her, peeping into the drawing room to say good night to Tallie and her beau. We did not like him much because he kissed us and was preachy when we cheeked pretty Tallie, who did not rule over us as Dede did; but he brought candy—chocolates for Tallie and a bag of "broken mixed" for the children, big hunky pieces that sucked you right into sleep.

Dede put Dick to bed. Lizzie had a room of her own. Alice and I shared. We undid each other and brushed our hair to long sweet suckings.

"I wish he'd come in the morning before church."

"What for?"

"Sunday'd be lots nicer if you could have a chunk of candy in your cheek all day."

"Stupid! Could you go to church with candy poking out of your cheek like another nose? Could you slobber candy over your Sunday School Lesson and the Bible reading?"

Alice was two years older than I. She stopped brushing her long red hair, jumped into bed, leaned over the chair that the candle sat on.

Pouf!. . . Out went Sunday and the candle.

The Cow Yard

THE COW YARD was large. Not length and breadth alone determined its dimensions, it had height and depth also. Above it continually hovered the spirit of maternity. Its good earth floor, hardened by many feet, pulsed with rich growth wherever there was any protection from the perpetual movement over its surface.

Across the ample width of the Cow Yard, the old Barn and the New Barn faced each other. Both were old, but one was very old; in it lodged the lesser creatures. The Cow alone occupied the New Barn.

But it was in the Cow Yard that you felt most strongly the warm life-giving existence of the great red-and-white, loose-knit Cow. When she walked, her great bag swung slowly from side to side. From one end of her large-hipped square body nodded a massive head, surmounted by long, pointed horns. From the other dangled her tail with its heavy curl and pendulum-like movement. As her cloven hoofs moved through the mud, they made a slow clinging squelch, all in tune with the bagging, sagging, nodding, leisureliness of the Cow's whole being.

Of the three little girls who played in the Cow Yard, Bigger tired of it soonest. Right through she was a pure, clean child, and had an enormous conscience. The garden rather than the Cow Yard suited her crisp frocks and tidy ways best, and she was a little afraid of the Cow.

Middle was a born mother, and had huge doll families. She liked equally the tidy garden and the free Cow Yard.

Small was wholly a Cow Yard child.

When the Cow's nose was deep in her bran mash, and her milk purring into the pail in long, even streams, first sounding tinny in the empty pail and then making a deeper and richer sound as the pail filled, Bong, sitting on his three-legged stool, sang to the Cow—a Chinese song in a falsetto voice. The Cow took her nose out of the mash bucket, threw back her great ears, and listened. She pulled a tuft of sweet hay from her rack, and stood quite still, chewing softly, her ears right about, so that she might not miss one bit of Bong's song.

One of the seven gates of the Cow Yard opened into the Pond Place. The Pond was round and deep, and the primroses and daffodils that grew on its bank leaned so far over to peep at themselves that some of them got drowned. Lilacs and pink and white may filled the air with sweetness in Spring. Birds nested there. The Cow walked on a wide walk paved with stones when she came to the Pond to drink. Hurdles of iron ran down each side of the walk and into the water, so that she should not go too far, and get mired. The three little girls who came to play used to roost on the hurdles and fish for tadpoles with an iron dipper that belonged to the hens' wheat-bin. From the brown surface of the water three upside-down little girls laughed up and mocked them, just as an upside-down Cow looked up from the water and mocked the Cow when she drank. Doubtless the tadpoles laughed, because down under the water where they darted back and forth no upside-down tadpoles mocked.

The overflow from the Pond meandered through the Cow Yard in a wide, rock-bordered ditch. There were two bridges across the ditch; one made of two planks for people to walk over, and the other made of logs, strong and wide enough for the Cow. The hens drank from the running water. Musk grew under the Cow's bridge; its yellow blossoms gleamed like cats' eyes in the cool dark.

Special things happened in the Cow Yard at each season of the year, but the most special things happened in Spring.

First came the bonfire. All winter the heap in the centre of the Cow Yard had mounted higher and higher with orchard prunings, branches that had blown down in the winter winds, old boxes and hens' nests, garbage, and now, on top of all, the spring-cleaning discards.

The three little girls sat on three upturned barrels. Even Bigger, her hands folded in a spotless lap, enjoyed this Cow Yard event. The Cow, safely off in the pasture, could not stamp and sway at her. Middle, hugging a doll, and Small, hugging a kitten, banged their heels on the sides of the hollow barrels, which made splendid noises like drums.

The man came from the barn with paper and matches, and off the bonfire blazed with a tremendous roar. It was so hot that the barrels had to be moved back. The hens ran helter-skelter. The rabbits wiggled their noses furiously as the whiffs of smoke reached their hutches. The ducks waddled off to the Pond to cool themselves. Soon there was nothing left of the bonfire but ashes and red embers. Then the barrels were rolled up close, and the three little girls roasted potatoes in the hot ashes.

Bigger told stories while the potatoes roasted. Her stories were grand and impossible, and when they soared beyond imagining, Small said, "Let's have some real ones now," and turned to Middle, "Will you marry?"

"Of course," came the prompt reply. "And I shall have a hundred children. Will you?"

Small considered. "Well, that depends. If I don't join a circus and ride a white horse through hoops of fire, I may marry a farmer, if he has plenty of creatures. That is, I wouldn't marry just a vegetable man."

"I am going to be a missionary," said Bigger, "and go out to the Heathen."

"Huh! if you're scared of our old cow, what will you be of cannibals?" said Small. "Why not marry a missionary, and send him out first, so they wouldn't be so hungry when you got there?"

"You are a foolish child," said Bigger. "The potatoes

17

are cooked. You fish them out, Small, your hands and pinafore are dirty anyway."

The ashes of the bonfire were scarcely cold before Spring burst through the brown earth, and the ashes and everything. The Cow and the chickens kept the tender green shoots cropped down, but every night more pushed up and would not be kept under. The Cow watched the willow trees that grew beside the Pond. Just before the silky grey pussies burst their buds, she licked up as far as she could reach and ate them, blowing hard, upside-down sniffs—all puff-out and no pull-in—as though the bitter-sweet of the pussy-willows was very agreeable to her. She stood with half-closed eyes, chewing and rolling her jaws from side to side, with delighted slobbering.

About this time, the fussy old hens got fussier. After sticking their feathers on end, and clucking and squawking and being annoyed at everybody, they suddenly sat down on their nests, and refused to get up, staring into space as though their orange eyes saw something away off. Then they were moved into a quiet shed and put into clean boxes of hollowed-out hay, filled with eggs. They sat on top of the eggs for ages and ages. If you put your hand on them, they flattened their feathers to their bodies and their bodies down on their eggs and gave beaky growls. Then, when you had almost forgotten that they ever had legs and could walk, you went to the shed and put food and water before them. Fluffy chickens peeped out of every corner of the hen's feathers, till she looked as fat as seven hens. Then she strutted out into the yard, to brag before the other creatures, with all the chicks bobbing behind her.

One old hen was delighted with her chickens and went off, clucking to keep them close, and scratching up grubs and insects for them by the way, but when they came to the ditch her little ones jumped into the water and swam off. She felt that life had cheated her, and she sat down and sulked.

"How mad she must be, after sitting so long," said Bigger.

"As long as they are alive, I don't see why she should care," said Middle. "They'll come to her to be cuddled when they are tired and cold."

"Oh, girls," cried Small, bursting with a big idea, "if the hen hatched ducks, why couldn't the Cow have a colt? It would be so splendid to have a horse!"

Bigger got up from the stone where she was sitting. "Come on," she said to Middle, "she is such a foolish child. Let's play ladies in the garden, and leave her to mudpuddle in the Cow Yard."

The ducklings crept back to the old hen when they were tired, just as Middle had said they would. The old hen squatted down delightedly, loosening up her feathers, and the little ducks snuggled among them.

"Aren't they beastly wet and cold against your skin?" shouted Small across the ditch to the hen. "Gee, don't mothers love hard!"

She cast a look around the yard. Through the fence she saw the Cow in the pasture, chewing drowsily. Spring sunshine, new grass, daisies and buttercups filled the pasture. The Cow had not a trouble in the world.

Small nodded to the Cow. "All the same, old Cow, I do wish you could do something about a colt. Oh dear, I do want to learn to ride!"

Suddenly she sprang up, jumped the ditch, tiptoed to reach the iron hoop that kept the pasture-gate fast, and ran up to the Cow. "Be a sport, old girl," she whispered in the great hairy ear, and taking her by the horn she led the Cow up to the fence.

The Cow stood meek and still. Small climbed to the top rail of the fence, and jumped on the broad expanse of red back, far too wide for her short legs to grip. For one still moment, while the slow mind of the Cow surmounted her astonishment, Small sat in the wide valley between horns and hip-bones. Then it seemed as though the Cow fell apart, and as if every part of her shot in a different direction.

Small hurled through space and bumped hard. "Beast!"

she gasped, when she had sorted herself from the mud and the stones. "Bong may call you the Old Lady, but I call you a mean, miserable old cow." And she shook her fist at the still-waving heels and tail at the other end of the pasture.

That night, when Small showed Middle the bruises, and explained how they had come, Middle said, "I expect you had better marry a farmer; maybe you're not exactly suited for a circus rider."

Spring had just about filled up the Cow Yard. The rabbits' secrets were all out now. They had bunged up the doors of their sleeping boxes with hay and stuff, and had pretended that there was nothing there at all. But if you went too close, they stamped their feet and wagged their ears, and made out that they were brave as lions. But now that it had got too stuffy in the boxes, the mother pulled down the barricade and all the fluffy babies scampered out, more than you could count.

One day when the Cow was standing under the loft, the loveliest baby pigeon fell plumb on her back. But there were so many young things around, all more or less foolish, that the Cow was not even surprised.

Then one morning the Father called the little girls into the Cow Yard, to see the pigmy image of the Old Cow herself, spot for spot, except that it had no wisdom. He had a foolish baby face and foolish legs; he seemed to wonder whose legs these were, and never dreamed that they were his own. But he was sure that he owned his tail, and flipped it joyously.

The Cow was terribly proud of him, and licked him and licked him till all his hair crinkled up.

Now, the Cow Yard was not Heaven, so of course bad things and sad things happened there too.

Close by the side of the ditch was a tree covered with ivy. The running water had washed some of the roots bare, and they stuck out. When the little girls sailed boats down the ditch, the roots tipped the boats and tried to drown the dolls.

It was not a very big tree, but the heavy bunch of ivy that hung about it made it look immense. The leaves of the ivy formed a dense dark surface about a foot away from the bole of the tree, for the leaves hung on long stems. The question was—what filled the mysterious space between the leaves and the tree? Away above the ivy, at the top, the bare branches of the tree waved skinny arms, as if they warned you that something terrible was there.

One day the children heard the Father say to the Mother, "The ivy has killed that tree."

It was strange that the ivy could kill anything. Small thought about it a lot, but she did not like to ask the older ones, who thought her questions silly. She would not have thrust her arm into that space for anything.

The pigeons flew over the tree, from the roof of one barn to the roof of the other, but they never lighted on it. Sometimes the noisy barn sparrows flew into the ivy; they were instantly silent, and you never saw them come out. Sometimes owls hoo-hoo-hooed in there. Once when Small was sitting on the chopping block, one flew out, perfectly silently, as though its business were very secret. Small crept home and up to bed, although it was not quite time, and drew the covers tight up over her head. To herself she called that tree "The Killing Tree".

Then one day she found a dead sparrow under the Killing Tree.

She picked it up. The bird was cold, its head flopped over her hand; the rest of it was stiff and its legs stuck up. Queer grey lids covered its eyes.

Small buried it in a little box filled with violets. A week later she dug it up, to see just what did happen to dead things. The bird's eyes were sunk away back in its head. There were some worms in the box, and it smelled horrid. Small buried the bird in the earth again quickly.

Winter came by and by and, looking out from their bedroom window, Middle said, "The Old Cow Yard tree is down." They dressed quickly and went to look.

The tree had broken the Cow's bridge and lay across

the ditch, the forlorn top broken and pitiful. The heavy ivy, looking blacker than ever against the snow, still hid the mystery place.

"Mercy, it's good it did not fall on the Cow and kill her," said Small. "It's a beastly tree and I'm glad it is down!"

"Why should it fall on the Cow; and why was it a beastly tree?" asked Middle.

"Because and because," said Small, and pressed her lips together tight.

"You *are* silly," retorted Middle.

When they came back from school, the top branches were chopped up, and the ivy piled ready for burning. The little tawny roots of the ivy stuck out all over the bole like coarse hair. The Man was sawing the tree in lengths. He rolled one towards the children. "Here's a seat for you," he said. Middle sat down. Small came close to the Man.

"Mr. Jack, when you chopped the ivy off the tree did you find anything in there?"

"Why, I found the tree."

"I mean," said Small in a tense voice, "anything between the tree and the ivy?"

"There wasn't nothing in there that I saw," replied the Man. "Did you lose a ball or something maybe?"

"When are you going to burn the ivy?"

"Just waiting till you came home from school," and he struck a match.

Dense, acrid smoke blinded the children. When they could see again, long tongues of flame were licking the leaves, which hissed back like a hundred angry cats, before they parched, crackled, and finally burst into flames.

"Isn't it a splendid bonfire?" asked Middle. "Shall we cook potatoes?"

"No," said Small.

The next spring, when everyone had forgotten that there ever had been a Cow Yard tree, the Father bought a horse. The Cow Yard was filled with excitement; children shouted, hens ran, ducks waddled off quacking, but the Cow did not even look up. She went right on eating some greens from a pile thrown over the fence from the vegetable garden.

"I suppose we shall have to call it the Horse Yard now," said Small. "He's bigger and so much grander than the Cow."

Middle gave the horse an appraising look. "Higher, but not so thick," she said.

The horse saw the pile of greens. He held his head high, and there was confidence in the ring of his iron shoes as he crossed the bridge.

The Cow munched on, flapping the flies off her sides with a lazy tail. When she got a particularly juicy green, her tail forgot to flap, and lay curled across her back.

When the horse came close, the tail jumped off the Cow's back and swished across his nose. He snorted and pulled back, but still kept his eyes on the pile of greens. He left his four feet and the tips of his ears just where they had been, but the roots of his ears, and his neck and lips stretched forward towards the greens till he looked as if he would fall for crookedness. The Cow's head moved ever so little; she gave him a look, and pointed one horn right at his eye. His body shot back to where it should be, square above his legs, and he sighed and turned away, with his ears and tail pressed down tight.

"I guess it will be all right for us to call it the Cow Yard still," said Middle.

The Bishop and the Canary

SMALL had earned the canary and loved him. How she did love him!

When they had told her, "You may take your pick," and she leaned over the cage and saw the four fluffy yellow balls, too young to have even sung their first song, her breath and her heart acted so queerly that it seemed as if she must strangle.

She chose the one with the topknot. He was the first live creature she had ever owned.

"Mine! I shall be his God," she whispered.

How could she time her dancing feet to careful stepping? She was glad the cage protected him sufficiently so that she could hug it without hurting him.

Save for the flowers that poked their faces through the fences, and for the sunshine, the long street was empty. She wished that there was someone to show him to—someone to say, "He *is* lovely!"

A gate opened and the Bishop stepped into the street. The Bishop was very holy—everybody said so. His eyes were blue, as if by his perpetual contemplation of Heaven they had taken its colour. His gentle voice, vague and distant, came from up there too. His plump hands were transparent against the clerically black vest.

Though she played ladies with his little girls, Small stood in great awe of the Bishop. She had never voluntarily addressed him. When they were playing in his house, the children tiptoed past his study. God and the Bishop were in there making new hymns and collects.

Her lovely bird! Because there was no one else to show **him** to she must show him to the Bishop. Birds belonged to the sky. The Bishop would understand. She was not at all afraid now. The bird gave her courage.

She ran across the street.

"Look, Bishop! Look at my bird!"

The Bishop's thoughts were too far away, he did not heed nor even hear the cry of joy.

She stood before him with the cage held high. "Bishop! Oh please Bishop, see!"

Dimly the Bishop became aware of some object obstructing his way. He laid a dimpled hand upon the little girl's head.

"Ah, child, you are a pretty picture," he said, and moved her gently from his path.

The Bishop went his way. The child stood still.

"My beautiful bird!"

The look of hurt fury which she hurled at the Bishop's back might have singed his clerical broadcloth.

The Blessing

FATHER'S religion was grim and stern, Mother's gentle. Father's operated through the Presbyterian, Mother's through the Anglican Church. *Our* religion was hybrid: on Sunday morning we were Presbyterian, Sunday evening we were Anglican.

Our little Presbyterian legs ached from the long walk to church on Sunday morning. Our hearts got heavy and our eyes tired before the Presbyterian prayers and the long Presbyterian sermon were over. Even so, we felt a strong "rightness" about Father's church which made it endurable. Through scorch of summer heat, through snow and rain, we all taggled along behind Father. Toothaches, headaches, stomach-aches—nothing was strong enough to dodge or elude morning religion.

Mother's religion was a Sunday evening privilege. The Anglican church was much nearer our house than the Presbyterian, just a little walk down over Marvin's Hill to our own James' Bay mud-flats. The little church sat on the dry rim just above the far side.

Evening service was a treat that depended on whether big sister wanted to be bothered with us. Being out at night was very special too—moon and stars so high, town lights and harbour lights low and twinkly when seen from the top of Marvin's Hill on our side of the mud-flats. A river of meandering sludge loitered its way through the mud —a huge silver snake that twisted among the sea-grass. On the opposite side of the little valley, on a rocky ridge, stood Christ Church Cathedral, black against the night-blue of the sky. Christ Church had chimes and played scales on them to walk her people to church. As we had no chimes, not even a bell on our church, we marched along on the spare noise of the Cathedral chimes.

The mud-flats did not always smell nice although the bushes of sweet-briar on the edge of the high-water rim did their best, and the sea crept in between the cafless wooden legs of James' Bay Bridge, washed the muddied grass and stole out again.

Our Church was mellow. It had a gentle, mild Bishop. He wore a long black gown with a long white surplice over it. His immense puffed sleeves were caught in at the wrists by black bands and fluted out again in little white frills round his wrists. There was a dimple on each knuckle of his hands. He was a wide man and looked wider in his surplice, especially from our pew, which was close up under the pulpit. He looked very high above us and every time he caught his breath his beard hoisted and waved out.

The Bishop's voice was as gentle as if it came from the moon. Every one of his sentences was separated from the next by a wheezy little gasp. His face was round and circled by a mist of white hair. He kept the lids shut over his blue, blue eyes most of the time, as if he was afraid their blueness would fade. When you stood before him you felt it was the lids of his own eyes he saw, not you.

The Bishop's favourite word was "Ah!", not mournful or vexed "ahs", just slow contemplating "ahs". But it was the Bishop's Blessing! He blessed most splendidly! From the moment you went into church you waited for it. You could nap through most of the Presbyterian sermon, but, although the pews were most comfortable, red cushions, footstool and all, you dared not nap through the Bishop's for fear you'd miss the blessing.

Our Evangelical church was beautiful. There was lots of music. A lady in a little red velvet bonnet, with strings under the chin, played the organ.

There were four splendid chandeliers dangling high under the roof. They had round, wide reflectors made of very shiny, very crinkly tin. Every crinkle caught its own particular bit of light and tossed it round the church—and up there ever so high the gas jets hissed and flickered. Music stole whispering from the organ and crept up among the chandeliers and the polished rafters to make echoes.

Our choir was mixed and sang in every sort of clothes, not in surplices like the Cathedral choir on the hill.

The Bishop climbed into the pulpit. He laid the sheets of his sermon on the open Bible which sat on a red velvet cushion; then he shut his eyes and began to preach. Once in a while he would stop, open his eyes, put on his glasses and read back to be sure he had not skipped.

When the last page was turned the Bishop said a gentle "Amen" and then he lifted his big round sleeves with his hands dangling out of the ends. We all stood up and drooped our heads. The church was full of stillness. The Bishop curved his palms out over us—they looked pink against his white sleeves. He gave the blessing just as if he was taking it straight from God and giving it to us.

Then the Bishop came down the pulpit stairs; the organ played and the choir sang him into the vestry; the verger nipped the side lights off in such a hurry that everyone fell over a footstool.

Big doors rolled back into the wall on either side of the church door to let us out. As soon as we were all in the night the verger rolled shut the doors and blotted out the chandeliers.

We climbed Marvin's Hill, each of us carrying home a bit of the Bishop's blessing.

Singing

SMALL'S singing was joyful noise more than music; what it lacked in elegance it made up in volume. As fire cannot help giving heat so Small's happiness could not help giving song, in spite of family complaint. They called her singing a "horrible row", and said it shamed them before the neighbours, but Small sang on. She sang in the cow-yard, mostly, not that she went there specially to sing, but she was so happy when she was there among the creatures that the singing did itself. She had but to open her mouth and the noise jumped out.

The moment Small sat down upon the cow-yard woodpile the big rooster would jump into her lap and the cow amble across the yard to plant her squareness, one leg under each corner, right in front of Small and, to shut out completely the view of the old red barn, the hen houses, and the manure-pile.

The straight outline of the cow's back in front of Small was like a range of mountains with low hills and little valleys. The tail end of the cow was as square as a box. Horns were her only curve—back, front, tail, neck and nose in profile, were all straight lines. Even the slobber dripping from her chin fell in slithery streaks.

When Small began to sing the old cow's nose-line shot from straight down to straight out, her chin rose into the air, her jaws rolled. The harder Small sang, the harder the cow chewed and the faster she twiddled her ears around as if stirring the song into the food to be rechewed in cud along with her breakfast.

Small loved her cow-yard audience—hens twisting their silly heads and clawing the earth with mincing feet, their down eye looking for grubs, their up eye peering at Small, ducks trying hard to out-quack the song, pigeons clapping their white wings, rabbits hoisting and sinking their noses— whether in appreciation or derision Small could never tell.

White fluttered through the cow-yard gate, Bigger's apron heralding an agitated Bigger, both hands wrestling with the buttons of her apron behind and her tongue ready sharpened to attack Small's singing.

"It's disgusting! Stop that vulgar row, Small! What must the neighbours think? Stop it, I say!"

Small sang harder, bellowing the words, "The cow likes it and this is her yard."

"I wish to goodness that she would roof her yard then, or that you would sing under an umbrella, Small, and so keep the sound down and not let it boil over the fences. There's the breakfast bell! Throw that fowl out of your lap and come! Song before breakfast means tears before night."

"Whose tears—mine, the cow's or the rooster's?"

"Oh, oh, oh! That cow-brute has dripped slobber down my clean apron! You're a disgusting pair," shrieked Bigger and rushed from the yard.

Breakfast over, the Elder detained Small.

"Small, this singing of yours is scandalous! Yesterday I was walking up the street with a lady. Half a block from our gate she stopped dead. 'Listen! Someone is in trouble,' she said. How do you think I felt saying, 'Oh, no, it is only my little sister singing'?"

Small reddened but said stubbornly, "The cow likes my singing."

Cows are different from humans; perhaps the hairiness of their ears strains sound.

The Bishop came to pay a sick-visit to Small's mother. He prayed and Small watched and listened. His deliberate chewing of the words, with closed eyes, reminded her of the cow chewing her cud. The Bishop was squarely built, a slow calm man. "They are very alike," thought Small.

Rising from his knees, the Bishop, aware of the little girl's stare, said, "You grow, child!"

"She does," said Small's mother. "So does her voice; her singing is rather a family problem."

"Song is good," replied Bishop. "Is it hymns you sing, child?"

"No, Mr. Bishop, I prefer cow-songs."

The Bishop's "a-a-h!" long drawn and flat lasted all the way down the stairs.

"You should not have said that," said Small's mother. "A Bishop is a Bishop."

"And a cow is a cow. Is it so wicked to sing to a cow?"

"Not wicked at all. I love your happy cow-yard songs coming into my window. We will have your voice trained some day. Then perhaps the others will not scold so much about your singing."

"But will the cow like my voice squeezed little and polite? It won't be half so much fun singing beautifully as boiling over like the jam kettle."

Small's four sisters and her brother went holidaying to a farm in Metchosin. Small was left at home with her mother. Just at first Small, to whom animal life was so dear, felt a pang that she was not of the farm party. But the quiet of the empty house was a new experience and something happened.

Mrs. Gregory, her mother's friend of long standing, came to spend an afternoon.

Both ladies were nearing the age of fifty—straightbacked, neatly made little ladies who sat primly on the horsehair chairs in the drawing-room wearing little lace-trimmed matron's caps and stitching each on a piece of plain sewing as they chatted.

Having exchanged recipes for puddings, discussed the virtue of red flannel as against white, the problem of Chinese help and the sewing-circle where they made brown holland aprons for orphans, all topics were exhausted.

They sewed in silence, broken after a bit by Mrs. Gregory saying, "There was English mail this morning, Emily. Do you ever get homesick for the Old Country?"

Small's mother looked with empty eyes across the garden. "My home and my family are here," she replied.

The ladies began "remembering". One would say, "Do you remember?" and the other would say, "I call to mind." Soon this remembering carried them right away from that Canadian drawing-room. They were back in Devonshire lanes, girl brides rambling along with their Richard and William, pausing now and then to gather primroses and to listen to the larks and cuckoos.

Small's mother said, "Richard was always one for wanting to see new countries."

"My William's hobby," said Mrs. Gregory, "was growing things. Here or there made no difference to him as long as there was earth to dig and flowers to grow."

Small knew that Richard and William were her Father and Mr. Gregory or she would never have recognized the ladies' two jokey boys of the Devonshire lanes in the grave middle-aged men she knew as her father and Mrs. Gregory's husband.

The ladies laid their sewing upon the table and, dropping their hands into their laps, sat idle, relaxing their shoulders into the hard backs of the chairs. Small felt it extraordinary to see them doing nothing, to see Canada suddenly spill out of their eyes as if a dam had burst and let the pent-up England behind drown Canada, to see them sitting in real chairs and yet not there at all.

The house was quite still. In the yard Bong was chopping kindling and droning a little Chinese song.

Suddenly Mrs. Gregory said, "Emily, let's sing!" and began:

"I cannot sing the old songs now I sang long years ago. . . ."

Small's mother joined, no shyness, no hesitation. The

two rusty little voices lifted, found to their amazement that they *could* sing the old songs still, and their voices got stronger and stronger with each song.

Sitting on a stool between them, half hidden by the table-cloth and entirely forgotten by the ladies, Small watched and listened, saw their still fingers, unornamented except for the plain gold band on the third left of each hand, lying in sober-coloured stuff-dress laps, little white caps perched on hair yet brown, lace jabots pinned under their chins by huge brooches. Mrs. Gregory's brooch was composed of tiny flowers woven from human hair grown on the heads of various members of her family. The flowers were glassed over the top and framed in gold, and there were earrings to match dangling from her ears. The brooch Small's mother wore was made of quartz with veins of gold running through it. Richard had dug the quartz himself from the California gold mines and had had it mounted in gold for his wife with earrings of the same.

Each lady had winds and winds of thin gold watch-chain round her neck, chains which tethered gold watches hiding in stitched pockets on the fronts of their dresses. There the ladies' hearts and their watches could tick duets.

Small sat still as a mouse. The singing was as solemn to her as church. She had always supposed that Mother-ladies stopped singing when there were no more babies in their nurseries to be sung to. Here were two ladies nearly fifty years old, throwing back their heads to sing love songs, nursery songs, hymns, God Save the Queen, Rule Britannia —songs that spilled over the drawing-room as easily as Small's cow songs spilled over the yard, only Small's songs were new, fresh grass snatched as the cow snatched pasture grass. The ladies' songs were rechews—cudded fodder.

Small sneezed!

Two mouths snapped like mousetraps! Four cheeks flushed! Seizing her sewing, Mrs. Gregory said sharply, "Hunt my thimble, child!"

Small's mother said, "I clean forgot the tea," and hurried from the room.

Small never told a soul about that singing but now, when she sat on the cow-yard woodpile she raised her chin and sang clean over the cow's back, over the yard and over the garden, straight into her mother's window ... let Bigger and the Elder scold!

The Praying Chair

THE WICKER chair was new and had a crisp creak. At a quarter to eight every morning Father sat in it to read family prayers. The little book the prayers came out of was sewed into a black calico pinafore because its own cover was a vivid colour and Father did not think that was reverent.

The Elder, a sister much older than the rest of the children, knelt before a hard, straight chair: Mother and little Dick knelt together at a low soft chair. The three little girls, Bigger, Middle, and Small usually knelt in the bay window and buried their faces in its cushioned seat but Small's Father liked her to kneel beside him sometimes. If she did not get her face down quickly he beckoned and Small had to go from the window-seat to under the arm of the wicker chair. It was stuffy under there. Small liked the window-seat best, where she could peep and count how many morning-glories were out, how many new rosebuds climbing to look in through the window at her.

Father's wicker chair helped pray. It creaked and whispered more than the children would ever have dared to. When finally Father leaned across the arm to reach for the cross-work book-mark he had laid on the table during prayers, the chair squawked a perfectly grand Amen.

One morning Father had a bit of gout and Small thought that instead of Amen Father said "Ouch!" She could not be quite sure because just at the very moment that the chair amened, Tibby, the cat, gave a tremendous "meow" and a splendid idea popped into Small's head.

Small had wanted a dog—she did not remember how long she had wanted it—it must have been from the beginning of the world. The bigger she got the harder she wanted.

As soon as everyone had gone about their day's business Small took Tibby and went back to the praying chair.

"Look, Tibby, let's you and me and the praying chair ask God to give you a puppy for me. Hens get ducks, why couldn't you get a puppy? Father always sits in that chair to pray. It must be a good chair; it amens splendidly. I'll do the words: you and the chair can amen. I don't mind what kind of a puppy it is as long as it's alive."

She tipped the chair and poked Tibby underneath into the cage-like base. Tibby left her tail out.

"So much the better," said Small. "It'll pinch when the time for amen is ready."

Tibby's amen was so effective that Small's Mother came to see what was the trouble.

"Poor cat! Her tail is pinched. Take her out into the garden, Small."

"It's all spoilt now!"

"What is?"

"We were praying for a puppy."

"Your Father won't hear of a puppy in his garden, Small."

Small's birthday was coming.

The Elder said, "I know something that is coming for your birthday!"

"Is it—is it—"

"Wait and see."

"Does it commence with 'd'? Or, if it's just a little one, maybe with 'p'?"

"I think it does."

The day before the great day Small's singing was a greater nuisance than usual. Everyone scolded till she danced off to the woodshed to sing there, selected three boxes of varying sizes and brushed them out.

"Which size will fit him? Middle, when you got your new hair-brush what did you do with the old one?"

"Threw it out."

Small searched the rubbish pile which was waiting for the Spring bonfire and found the brush-back with its few remaining bristles.

"A lot of brushing with a few is as good as a little brushing with a lot. . ."

"Rosie," she said to the wax doll whose face had melted smooth because a mother, careless of dead dolls, had left her sitting in the sun, "Rosie, I shall give your woollie to my new pup. You are all cold anyhow. You melt if you are warmed. Pups are live and shivery. . ."

"He . . . she . . . Oh, Rosie, what *shall* I do if it's a she? It took years to think up a good enough name and it's a boy's name. Oh, well, if it's a girl she'll have thousands of puppies; the Elder says they always do."

She plaited a collar of bright braid, sewing on three hooks and eyes at varying distances.

"Will he be so big—or so big—or so big? I don't care about his size or shape or colour as long as he's alive."

She put the collar into the pocket of tomorrow's clean pinafore.

"Hurry up and go, day, so that tomorrow can come!" And she went off to bed so as to hurry night.

Small's father drew back the front-door bolt; that only half unlocked the new day—the little prayer book in its drab covering did the rest. It seemed a terrible time before the chair arm squeaked Amen. The Elder rose, slow as a snail. Small wanted to shout, "Hurry, hurry! Get the pup for me!"

Everyone kissed Small for her birthday; then all went into the breakfast room. On Small's plate was a flat, flat parcel. Small's eyes filled, drowning the gladness.

"Open it!" shouted everyone.

The Elder cut the string. "I am glad to see," she remarked, noting Small's quivering blue hands, "that you did not shirk your cold bath because it was your birthday."

The present was the picture of a little girl holding a dog in her arms.

"She looks like you," said Middle.

"No, she isn't like me, she has a dog."

Small went to the fire pretending to warm her blue hands. She took something from her apron pocket, dropped it into the flames.

"I'm not hungry—can I go and feed my ducks?" In the cow-yard she could cry.

The birthday dawdled. Small went to bed early that night too.

"Small, you forgot your prayers!" cried Bigger.

"I didn't—God's deaf."

"You're dreadfully, dreadfully wicked—maybe you'll die in the night."

"Don't care."

Years passed. Small's father and mother were dead. The Elder was no more reasonable than Small's father had been about dogs. Small never asked now, but the want was still there, grown larger. Bigger, Middle and Small were grown up, but the Elder still regarded them as children, allowed them no rights. Like every girl Small built castles in the air. Her castle was an ark, her man a Noah, she tended the beasts.

Unexpected as Amen in a sermon's middle came Small's dog. She had been away for a long, long time; on her return the Elder was softened. Wanting to keep Small home, she said, "There's a dog in the yard for you."

Dabbing a kiss on the Elder's cheek Small rushed. Kneeling she took the dog's muzzle between her hands. He sniffed, licked, accepted. Maybe he too had waited for a human peculiarly his. She loosed him. He circled round and round. Was he scenting the dream-pup jealously?

He had been named already. The dream-pup would always keep the name that had been his for his own.

"He'll run away—chain him. Remember he must not come in the house, Small!"

Small roamed beach and woods, the dog with her always. Owning him was better even than she had dreamed.

Small sat on a park bench waiting for a pupil, the dog asleep at her feet. The child-pupil, planning a surprise for Small, stole up behind her and threw her arms round her neck. Small screamed. The dog sprang, caught the child's arm between his teeth, made two tiny bruises and dropped down—shamed.

"That dog is vicious," said the Elder.

"Oh, no, he thought someone was hurting me; he was dreadfully ashamed when he saw that it was a child."

"He must be kept chained."

Chickens for table use were killed close to the dog's kennel. He smelled the blood—heard their squawks. The maid took a long feather and tickled his nose with it. He sprang, caught the girl's hand instead of the feather. The Elder's mouth went hard and grim.

"I teased him beyond endurance," pleaded the maid.

That day Small was hurt in an accident. The dog was not allowed to go to her room. Broken-hearted he lay in his kennel, disgraced, forsaken. Small was sent away to an old friend to recuperate. The day before she was to return, the old lady's son came to Small blurting, "They've killed your dog."

"Cruel, unjust, beastly!" shrieked Small.

"Hush!" commanded the old lady. "The dog was vicious."

"He was not! He was not! Both times he was provoked!"

Small ran and ran across fields till she dropped face down among the standing grain. There was a dark patch on the earth where her tears fell among roots of the grain.

"Only a dog! This is wrong, Small," said the not-understanding old woman.

Small went home and for six weeks spoke no word to the Elder—very few to anybody. She loathed the Elder's hands; they made her sick. Finally the Elder lost patience. "I did not kill the vicious brute," she cried. "The police shot him."

"You made them!"

Small could look at the Elder's hands again.

Small was middle-aged; she built a house. The Elder had offered her another dog. "Never till I have a home of my own," she had said. The Elder shrugged.

Now that Small had her house, the Elder criticized it. "Too far forward," she said. "You could have a nice front garden."

"I wanted a large back yard."

"A glut of dogs, eh Small?"

"A kennel of Bobtail Sheep dogs."

The Elder poked a head, white now, into Small's puppy nursery. "What are you doing, Small?"

"Bottling puppies—too many for the mothers."

"Why not bucket them?"

"There is demand for them—sheep dogs—cattle dogs."

"How many pups just now?"

"Eve's eight, Rhoda's seven, Loo's nine."

"Twenty-four—mercy! and, besides, those absurd bearded old patriarchs—Moses, Adam and the rest."

"Open the door for Adam."

The kennel sire entered, shaggy, noble, majestic. He rested his chin a moment on Small's shoulder where she sat with pup and feeding bottle, ran his eye round the walls where his mates and their families cuddled in boxes. He embraced all in good fellowship, including the Elder, picked the sunniest spot on the nursery floor and sprawled out.

"Oh, Small, I was throwing out Father's old wicker chair. Would you like it in the kennel nursery to sit in while bottling the pups?"

"The praying chair?—Oh, yes."

So the Praying Chair came to Small's kennel. Sitting in it Small remembered Tibby, the picture pup, the want, her first dog. Adam rested his chin on the old chair's arm. Small leaned forward to rest her cheek against his woolly head. All rasp, all crispness gone, "Amen", whispered the Praying Chair.

Mrs. Crane

I HEARD two women talking. One said to the other, "Mrs. Crane has a large heart."

"Yes," replied her companion, "and it is in the right place too."

I thought, "That's queer—hearts are in the middle of people. How can any person know if another person's heart is big or small, or if it is in the right or the wrong place?"

Soon after I heard this conversation about Mrs. Crane's heart, our Mother was seized with a very serious illness. My sister Alice and I—she was two years older—were hushed into the garden with our dolls and there, peeping from behind the currant bushes, we saw a high yellow dog-cart stop in front of our gate. Mrs. Crane descended from it and came stalking up our garden walk.

"Come to enquire, I s'pose," whispered Alice.

"My! Isn't she long and narrow?" I replied.

Silently I fell to trying to make all the different hearts I knew fit into Mrs. Crane's body—the gold locket one that made your neck shiver, beautiful valentine ones with for-get-me-nots around them, sugar hearts, with mottoes, a horrible brown thing Mother said was a pig's heart and boiled for the cat—none of these would fit into Mrs. Crane's long narrow body.

She seemed to grow taller and taller as she came nearer. When she tiptoed up the steps, to us, crouched behind the currant bushes, she seemed a giant.

My big sister opened the door to Mrs. Crane. They

whispered. Then my sister came to us and said, "Children, kind Mrs. Crane is going to take you home with her until Mother is better."

Alice's big eyes darkened with trouble. Obediently she picked up her doll and turned towards the house. I set my doll down with a spank, planted my feet wide apart and said, "Don't want to go!"

My sister gave me an impatient shake. Mrs. Crane ahem-med.

We were scrubbed hard, and buttoned into our starchiest. Mrs. Crane took one of Alice's hands and one of mine into a firm black kid grip and marched us to the gate. While she opened the gate, she let go of Alice's hand but doubled her grip on mine. Her eyes were like brown chocolate drops, hot and rich in colour when she looked at Alice, but when she looked at me they went cold and stale-looking.

We were hoisted up to the back seat of the dogcart. Father's splendid carpet bag with red roses on its sides and the great brass lock, was put under our feet to keep them from dangling. The bag was full of clean frocks and handkerchiefs and hairbrushes.

Mrs. Crane climbed up in front beside Mr. Crane. His seat was half a storey higher than hers. Mr. Crane cracked his whip and the yellow wheels spun furiously. Our house got smaller and smaller, then the road twisted and it was gone altogether. The world felt enormous.

We crossed two bridges. Mud flats were under one and the gas works were under the other—they both smelt horrid. The horse's hoofs made a deafening clatter on the bridges, and then they pounded steadily on and on over the hard road. When at last we came to the Crane's house, it seemed as if we must have gone all around the world, and then somehow got there hind-before. You passed the Crane's back gate first, and then you came to the front gate. The front door was on the back of the house. The house faced the water, which looked like a river, but was really the sea and salt. You went down the hill to the house and up the hill to the stable; everything was backwards to what it was at home and made you feel like Mother's egg-timer turned over.

Mrs. Crane had three little girls. The two younger were the same age as Alice and I.

The three little Cranes ran out of the house when they heard us come. They kissed Mama politely and, falling on Papa, hugged him like bears.

A man came to lead the horse away. The little Cranes were all busy guessing what was in the parcels that came from under the seat of the dogcart, but the receding clop! clop! of the horse's hoofs, hammered desolation into the souls of Alice and me.

The Crane's hall was big and warm and dark, except for the glow from a large heater, which pulled out shiny things like the noses of a lot of guns hanging in a rack on the wall and the fire irons and the stair rods. It picked out the brass lock of Father's bag and the poor glassy eyes of stuffed bear and wolves and owls and deer. Helen saw me looking at them as we went upstairs and said, "My Papa shot all those."

"What for?"

Helen stared at me. "What for? Doesn't your Papa go in for sport?"

"What is sport, Helen?"

Helen considered. "Why it's—killing things just for fun, not because you are hungry, chasing things with dogs and shooting them."

"My Father does not do that."

"My Papa is a crack shot," boasted Helen.

Alice and I had a grown-up bedroom. One window looked over the water and had a window seat. The other window looked into a little pine wood. There was a pair of beautiful blue china candlesticks on the mantel-piece.

We children had nursery tea. Mrs. Crane had Grace the biggest girl pour tea and Grace was snobbish. After tea we went into the drawing-room.

Mrs. Crane's drawing-room was a most beautiful room.

There was a big three-cornered piano in it, two sofas and a lot of lazy chairs for lolling in. At home only Father and Mother sat in easy chairs: they did not think it was good for little girls to sit on any kind but straight up-and-down chairs of wood or cane. Mrs. Crane's lazy chairs were fat and soft and were dressed up in shiny stuff with rosebuds sprinkled all over it. But bowls of real roses everywhere made the cloth ones look foolish and growing ones poking their pink faces into the open windows were best of all and smelled lovely. A bright little fire burned in the grate and kept the little sea breeze from being too cold and the breeze kept the fire from being too hot. In front of the fire was a big fur rug; a brown-and-white dog was sprawled out upon it.

When we five little girls trooped into the drawing-room, I thought that the dog was the only creature in the room. Then I saw the top of Mr. Crane's head and his slippers sticking out above and below a mound of newspapers in an easy chair on one side of the fire. On the other side the fire lit up Mrs. Crane's hands folded in her lap. Her face was hidden behind a beaded drape hanging from a brass rod which shaded her eyes from the fire-light. One hand lifted and patted a stool at her knee—this Helen went and sat on. Mrs. Crane's lap was deep and should have been splendid to sit in, but her little girls never sat there. Helen said it was because Mama's heart was weak and I said, "But Helen, I thought big things were always strong?"

Helen did not know what I meant, because of course she had not heard those ladies discussing her Mother's heart and so she did not know what I knew about it.

Mrs. Crane told "Gracie dear", to play one of her "pieces" on the piano. She always added dear to her children's names as if it was a part of them.

Mary Crane and our Alice were shy little girls. They sat on the sofa with their dolls in their laps. Their eyes stared like the doll's eyes. Mrs. Crane would not allow dolls to be dressed or undressed in the drawing-room; she said it was not nice. I sat on the edge of a chair till it tipped, then

I found myself in the very best place in all the room—right down on the fur rug beside the dog. When I put my head down on his side, he thumped his tail and a lovely live quiver ran through his whole body. I had meant to fight off sleep because of that strange bed upstairs, but the fire was warm and the dog comforting ... I couldn't think whose far-off voice it was saying, "Come to bed, children," or whose hand it was shaking me.

The cold upstairs woke us up. Mrs. Crane looked black and tall standing by the mantel-piece lighting the blue candles. The big room ran away into dark corners. The bed was turned down and our nighties were ready, but we did not seem to know what to do next unless it was to cry. Mrs. Crane did not seem to know what to do either, so she said, "Perhaps you little girls would like to come into my little girls' room while they undress?" So we sat on their ottoman and watched. They brushed themselves a great deal—their hair and nails and teeth. They folded their clothes and said their prayers into Mrs. Crane's front, then stepped into bed very politely. Mrs. Crane told them to lie on their right sides, keep their mouths shut and breathe through their noses, then she threw the windows up wide. The wind rushed in, sputtered the candle and swept between Mrs. Crane's kisses and the children's foreheads. Then she blew the candle gently as if she was trying to teach the wind manners.

Back in our room, Mrs. Crane said something about "undoing buttons". I backed up to Alice very quickly and she told Mrs. Crane that we could undo each other.

"Very well," said Mrs. Crane, "I'll come back and put out the candle presently."

We scurried into bed, pulled the covers up over our heads and lay very still.

She came and stood beside the two white mounds for a second—then two gentle puffs, the up-screech of the window, long soft footsteps receding down the hall.

Two heads popped up from the covers.

"Weren't you scared she'd kiss us?"

"Awfully! Or that she'd want to hear our prayers?"

"The Crane girls are very religious."

"How'd you know?"

"They said two verses of 'Now I lay me'. We only know one."

Alice always slept quickly and beautifully. I tossed every way and did not sleep, till all my troubles were pickled away in tears.

At breakfast while Mrs. Crane was busy with the teacups I got the first chance of staring at her hard. The light was good and she was much lower, sitting. She talked to Mr. Crane as she poured the tea, using big polite words in a deep voice. The words rolled round her wisdom teeth before they came out. Her hair, skin and dress were brown like her eyes. Her heart could not help being in the right place, it was clasped so tight by her corset and her brown stuff dress was stretched so taut above that and buttoned from chin to waist. Her heart certainly could not be a wide one. Her hands were clean and strong, with big knuckles. The longer I looked at Mrs. Crane the less I liked her. But I did like a lot of her things—the vase in the middle of the dining-room table for instance. Helen called it Mama's "epergne". It was a two-storey thing of glass and silver and was always full of choice flowers, pure white geraniums that one longed to stroke and kiss to see if they were real, fat begonias and big heavy-headed fuchsias. Flowers loved Mrs. Crane and grew for her.

Mrs. Crane's garden was not as tidy as Father's but the flowers had a good time and were not so prim. Mrs. Crane was lenient with her flowers. She let the wild ones scramble up and down each side of the clay path that ran down the bank to the sea. They jumbled themselves up like dancers— roses and honeysuckle climbed everywhere. The front drive, which was really behind the house, was circular and enclosed a space filled with fruit trees and raspberry canes. The vegetable garden was in the front and the flowerbeds in the back, because, of course, the front of the house was at the back. There was a little croquet lawn too and the little pine wood that our bedroom looked out on.

In the middle of this wood was a large platform with lots of dog-kennels on it—to these Mr. Crane's hunting dogs were chained.

The dogs did not know anything about women or girls and Mrs. Crane did not like them. Mr. Crane would not let the children handle them; he said it spoilt them for hunting. I wanted to go to them dreadfully but Helen said that I must not. The children were allowed to have the old one who had been in the drawing-room because he was no good for hunting.

Helen said, "Once I had a little black dog. I loved him very much, but Papa said he was a mongrel. So he got his gun and shot him. When the little dog saw the gun pointed at him he sat up and begged. The shot went through his heart, but he still sat up with the beg frozen in his paws."

"Oh Helen, how could your father? Why didn't your mother stop him?"

"It did not make any difference to Mama. It was not her dog."

In our house nobody would have thought of telling Father "not to". Nor would we have thought of meddling with Father's things. In the Cranes' home it was different. When Helen took me into a funny little room built all by itself in the garden and said, "This is Papa's Den," I was frightened and said, "Oh Helen! surely we ought not to."

There was not a single woman's thing in the Den. There were guns and fishing rods and wading boots and there was a desk with papers and lots of big books. There was a bottle of quicksilver. Helen uncorked it and poured it onto the table. It did amazing things, breaking itself to bits and then joining itself together again, but presently it rolled off the table and we could not find it. Whenever Mr. Crane came home after that, I was in terror for fear he would ask about the quicksilver and I hated him because he had shot the little begging dog.

The little Cranes never took liberties with Mama's things.

It seemed years since we left home, but neither Alice nor I had had a birthday and there had been only one Sunday at Mrs. Crane's. There was one splendid thing though and that was Cricket. He was a pinto pony belonging to the children. Every day he was saddled and we rode him in turns. The older girls rode in a long habit. Helen's legs and mine were too young to be considered improper by Mrs. Crane. So our frillies flapped joyously. Helen switched Cricket to make him go fast, but fast or slow were alike to me. It was a delight to feel his warm sides against my legs. The toss of his mane, the switch of his tail, his long sighs and short snorts, the delicious tickle of his lips when you fed him sugar—everything about him was entrancing, even the horsy smell. Just the thought of Cricket, when you were crying yourself to sleep, helped.

There was no more room for Cricket in Mrs. Crane's heart than there was for the dogs, but Mrs. Crane's heart did take in an old lady called Mrs. Miles. Mrs. Miles was almost deaf and almost blind. She wore a lace cap and a great many shawls and she knitted and blinked, knitted and blinked, all day. She came to stay with Mrs. Crane while we were there. Mrs. Miles liked fresh raspberries for her breakfast and to make up for being nearly blind and nearly deaf, Mrs. Crane gave her everything she could that she was fond of. We children had to get up earlier to pick raspberries and Mrs. Crane did not even mind if our fresh frocks got wetted with dew, because she wanted to comfort Mrs. Miles for being old and deaf and blind.

On Sunday afternoon Mrs. Miles draped her fluffiest shawl over her cap and face and everything and presently big snores came straining through it. Mr. Crane's newspaper was sitting on top of his bald spot and he was snoring too— the paper flapped in and out above his mouth. Mr. Crane's "awk, awk" and Mrs. Miles' "eek, eek" wouldn't keep step and we little girls giggled.

Mrs. Crane said, "It is very rude for little girls to laugh at their elders."

Helen asked, "Even at their snores, Mama?"

"Even at their snores," said Mrs. Crane. She hushed us into the far corner of the drawing-room and read us a very dull story.

Helen on the stool at her mother's knee and the three others on the sofa were all comfortable enough to shut their eyes and forget, but how could anyone on a three-legged stool under the high top of the sofa sleep? Especially if the fringe of an antimacassar lolled over the top and tickled your neck? My fingers reached up to the little tails of wool bunched in colours and began to plait—red, yellow, black, red, yellow, black. A neat little row of pigtails hung there when the story was done and I thought it looked fine.

When we trooped down the stairs next morning, Mrs. Crane was waiting at the foot. Her teeth looked very long, the chocolate of her eyes very stale. From the upper landing we must have looked like a long caterpillar following her to the drawing-room.

Of course she knew it was me, because she had told me to sit there, but she put me through five separate agonies, her pointing finger getting longer and her voice deeper, with every "Did you do it?" When it came to me, her finger touched the antimacassar and her voice dragged me into a deep pit. When I said my, "Yes, Mrs. Crane," she said that I had desecrated the work of her dear dead mother's hands, that it was Satan that had told my idle fingers to do it, that I was a naughty mischievous child and that after breakfast I must undo all the little pigtails.

Not the boom of the breakfast gong, nor the bellow of Mr. Crane's family prayers, nor the leather cushion that always smelt so real and nice when your nose went into it, could drown those horrid sobs. They couldn't be swallowed nor would they let my breakfast pass them. So Mrs. Crane excused me and I went to the beastly antimacassar and wished her mother had taken it to Heaven with her. Mrs.

Miles came and sat near and blinked and clicked, blinked and clicked.

"Please! Please! Mrs. Crane, can't we go home?"

"And make your poor Mama worse?"

I did not even want to ride Cricket that day.

After tea we went to visit a friend of Mrs. Crane's. We went in the boat. Mr. Crane rowed. Night came. Under the bridges the black was thick and the traffic thundered over our heads. Then we got into a boom of loose logs. They bumped our boat and made it shiver and when Mr. Crane stood up and pushed them away with his oar, it tipped. Helen and I were one on each side of Mrs. Crane in the stern. When she pulled one tiller rope her elbow dug into me, when she pulled the other her other elbow dug into Helen.

The ropes rattled in and out and the tiller squeaked. I began to shake and my teeth to chatter.

"Stop it, child!" said Mrs. Crane.

But I could not stop. I stared down into the black water and shook and shook and was deadly cold.

Mrs. Crane said I must have taken a chill. I had not eaten anything all day, so she gave me a large dose of castor oil when we got home. I felt dreadfully bad, especially in bed, when Alice said, "Why can't you behave? You've annoyed Mrs. Crane all day."

"I hate her! I hate her!" I cried. "She's got a pig's heart."

Alice said, "For shame!"—hitched the bedclothes over her shoulder and immediately long breaths came from her.

Next morning was wet, but about noon there was meek sunshine and Helen and I were sent to run up and down the drive.

Everything was so opposite at Mrs. Crane's that sometimes you had to feel your head to be sure you were not standing on it. For instance you could do all sorts of things in the garden, climb trees and swing on gates. It was not even wicked to step on a flower bed. But it was naughty to play in the stable yard among the creatures, or to tumble in the hay in the loft, or to lift a chicken, or to hold a puppy. Every time we came to the stable end of the drive, I just *had* to stop and talk to Cricket through the bars and peer into his great big eyes and whisper into his ears.

In the yard behind Cricket I saw a hen.

"Oh Helen, just look at that poor hen! How bad she does feel!"

"How do you know she feels bad?"

"Well, look at her shut eyes and her head and tail and wings all flopped. She feels as I did yesterday. Maybe oil. . ."

"I'll pour if you'll hold," said Helen.

We took the hen to the nursery. She liked the holding, but was angry at the pouring. When her throat was full she flapped free. I did not know a hen could fly so high. She knocked several things over and gargled the oil in her throat, then her big muddy feet clutched the top of the bookcase and she spat the oil over Mrs. Crane's books so that she could cackle. She had seemed so meek and sick we could not believe it. I was still staring when I heard a little squashed "Mama" come from Helen, as if something had crushed it out of her.

Sometimes I have thought that Mrs. Crane had the power to grow and shrivel at will. She filled the room, her eyes burnt and her voice froze.

"Catch that fowl!"

As I mounted the chair to catch the hen, I saw what her muddy feet and the oil had done to me. Helen's hair was long and she could hide behind it, but mine was short. I stepped carefully over the hateful blue bottle oozing sluggishly over the rug.

Out on the drive I plunged my burning face down into the fowl's soft feathers.

"Oh, old hen, I wish I could shrivel and get under your wing!" I cried. I had to put her down and go back alone.

It seemed almost as if I had shrivelled, I felt so shamed and small when I saw Mrs. Crane on her knees scrubbing the rug.

I went close. "I'm sorry, Mrs. Crane."

No answer. I went closer. "I wanted to help your hen. She's better. Perhaps it was only a little cuddling she wanted."

Oh, why didn't she speak! Why didn't she scold or even smack, not just scrub, scrub, scrub!

I stood looking down at Mrs. Crane. I had never seen the top of her before. I saw the part of her hair, the round of her shoulders, her broad back, her thickness when you saw her from on top. Perhaps after all there was room for quite a wide heart.

Suddenly now while I could reach her, I wanted to put my arms round her and cry.

Mrs. Crane rose so suddenly that she almost trod on me. I stepped back. The wings of her nose trembled. Mrs. Crane was smelling.

She strode to the doll cupboard and doubled down into it. When she backed out, a starfish dangled from the tips of the fingers of each hand. Helen and I had caught some under the boathouse ten days before and dressed them up in doll's clothes. Mrs. Crane's nose and hands were as far as they could get away from each other.

Mrs. Crane looked at me hard. "Such things never enter my Helen's head," she said. "Your mama is better; they are coming for you tonight."

In spite of the bad-smell-nose she wore, and the disgust in her fingertips, Mrs. Crane seemed to me just then a most beautiful woman.

"Oh, Mrs. Crane!"

My hands trembled up in that silly way pieces of us have of doing on their own, but the rest of me pulled them down quickly before Mrs. Crane saw.

White Currants

IT HAPPENED many times, and it always happened just in that corner of the old garden.

When it was going to happen, the dance in your feet took you there without your doing anything about it. You danced through the flower garden and the vegetable garden till you came to the row of currant bushes, and then you danced down it.

First came the black currants with their strong wild smell. Then came the red currants hanging in bright tart clusters. On the very last bush in the row the currants were white. The white currants ripened first. The riper they got, the clearer they grew, till you could almost see right through them. You could see the tiny veins in their skins and the seeds and the juice. Each currant hung there like an almost-told secret.

Oh! you thought, if the currants were just a wee bit clearer, then perhaps you could see them *living*, inside.

The white currant bush was the finish of the garden, and after it was a little spare place before you came to the fence. Nobody ever came there except to dump garden rubbish.

Bursting higgledy-piggledy up through the rubbish everywhere, grew a half-wild mauvy-pink flower. The leaves and the blossoms were not much to look at, because it poured every drop of its glory into its smell. When you went there the colour and the smell took you and wrapped you up in themselves.

The smell called the bees and the butterflies from ever

so far. The white butterflies liked it best; there were millions of them flickering among the pink flowers, and the hum of the bees never stopped.

The sun dazzled the butterflies' wings and called the smell out of the flowers. Everything trembled. When you went in among the mauvy-pink flowers and the butterflies you began to tremble too; you seemed to become a part of it—and then what do you think happened? Somebody else was there too. He was on a white horse and he had brought another white horse for me.

We flew round and round in and out among the mauvy-pink blossoms, on the white horses. I never saw the boy; he was there and I knew his name, but who gave it to him or where he came from I did not know. He was different from other boys, you did not have to see him, that was why I liked him so. I never saw the horses either, but I knew that they were there and that they were white.

In and out, round and round we went. Some of the pink flowers were above our heads with bits of blue sky peeping through, and below us was a mass of pink. None of the flowers seemed quite joined to the earth—you only saw their tops, not where they went into the earth.

Everything was going so fast—the butterflies' wings, the pink flowers, the hum and the smell, that they stopped being four things and became one most lovely thing, and the little boy and the white horses and I were in the middle of it, like the seeds that you saw dimly inside the white currants. In fact, the beautiful thing *was* like the white currants, like a big splendid secret getting clearer and clearer every moment—just a second more and——.

"Come and gather the white currants," a grown-up voice called from the vegetable garden.

The most beautiful thing fell apart. The bees and the butterflies and the mauvy-pink flowers and the smell, stopped being one and sat down in their own four places. The boy and the horses were gone.

The grown-up was picking beans. I took the glass dish.

"If we left the white currants, wouldn't they ripen a little more? Wouldn't they get—clearer?"

"No, they would shrivel."

"Oh!"

Then I asked, "What is the name of that mauvy-pink flower?"

"Rocket."

"Rocket?"

"Yes—the same as fireworks."

Rockets! Beautiful things that tear up into the air and burst!

The Orange Lily

HENRY MITCHELL's nursery garden was set with long rows of trees, shrubs and plants. It sat on the edge of the town. In one corner of its acreage was the little grey cottage where Henry and his wife, Anne, lived. They were childless and well on in years, trying honestly to choke down homesickness and to acclimatize themselves as well as their Old Country plants to their step-land.

Small came into the nursery garden taking the gravel path at a gallop, the steps at a jump, tiptoeing to reach the doorbell—then she turned sharp against the temptation of peering through the coloured glass at the door-sides to see sombre Anne Mitchell come down the hall multicoloured— green face, red dress, blue hair. The turn brought Small face to face with the Orange Lily.

The lily grew in the angle made by the front of the house and the side of the porch. Small's knees doubled to the splintery porch floor. She leaned over to look into the lily's trumpet, stuck out a finger to feel the petals. They had not the greasy feel of the wax lilies they resembled, they had not the smooth hard shininess of china. They were cool, slippery and alive.

Lily rolled her petals grandly wide as sentinelled doors roll back for royalty. The entrance to her trumpet was guarded by a group of rust-powdered stamens—her powerful perfume pushed past these. What was in the bottom of Lily's trumpet? What was it that the stamens were so carefully guarding? Small pushed the stamens aside and looked. The trumpet was empty—the emptiness of a church after parson and people have gone, when the music is asleep in the organ and the markers dangle from the Bible on the lectern.

Anne Mitchell opened the cottage door.

"Come see my everlasting flowers, Small—my flowers that never die."

With a backward look Small said, "What a lovely lily!"

"Well enough but strong-smelling, gaudy. Come see the everlastings."

The front room of the cottage was empty; newspapers were spread over the floor and heaped with the crisping everlasting flowers, each colour in a separate pile. The sunlight in the room was dulled by drawn white blinds. The air was heavy—dead, dusty as the air of a hay loft.

The flowers crackled at Anne's touch. "Enough to wreathe the winter's dead," she said with a happy little sigh and, taking a pink bud from the pile, twined it in the lace of her black cap. It dropped against her thin old cheek that was nearly as pink, nearly as dry as the flower.

"Come, Mrs. Gray's wreath!" She took Small to the sitting-room. Half of Mrs. Gray's wreath was on the table, Anne's cat, an invalid guinea hen and Henry huddled round the stove. The fire and the funereal everlastings crackled cheerfully.

Presently Small said, "I had better go now."

"You shall have a posy," said Anne, laying down the wreath.

"Will there be enough for Mrs. Gray and me too?" asked Small.

"We will gather flowers from the garden for you."

The Orange Lily! Oh if Mrs. Mitchell would only give me the Orange Lily! Oh, if only I could hold it in my hand and look and look!

Anne passed the lily. Beyond was the bed of pinks—white, clove, cinnamon.

"Smell like puddings, don't they?" said Small.

"My dear!"

Anne's scissors chawed the wiry stems almost as sapless

as the everlastings. Life seemed to have rushed to the heads of the pinks and flopped them face down to the ground. Anne blew off the dust as she bunched the pinks. Small went back to the lily. With pocket-handkerchief she wiped the petals she had rusted by pushing aside the stamens.

"There are four more lilies to come, Mrs. Mitchell!"

Anne lifted the corner of her black silk apron.

"That lily has rusted your nose, Small."

She scrubbed.

Small went home.

"Here's pinks," she said, tossing the bunch upon the table.

In her heart she hugged an Orange Lily. It had burned itself there not with flaming petals, not through the hot, rich smell. Soundless, formless, white—it burned there.

How Lizzie Was Shamed Right Through

NOW THAT I am eight, the same age that Lizzie was when the party happened, and am getting quite near to being grown-up, I can see how shamed poor Lizzie must have been of me then.

Now I know why the Langleys, who were so old, gave a party for us who were so little, but then I was only four so I did not wonder about it at all, nor notice that the fair, shy boy was their own little brother, hundreds and hundreds of years younger than his big brother and two big sisters. They did not poke his party in the little boy's face, did not say, "Albert, this is your party. You must be kind and polite to the boys and girls." That would have made Albert shyer than he was already. They let him enjoy his own party just as the other children were enjoying it.

The Langleys' party was the first one we had ever been to. Mother made us look very nice. We had frilly white dresses, very starched. Lizzie who was eight, and Alice who was six, had blue sashes and hair ribbons. There was pink ribbon on me and I was only four.

Sister Dede bustled round saying, "Hurry! Hurry!" scrubbing finger nails and polishing shoes. She knotted our ribbons very tightly so that we should not lose them,— they pulled the little hairs under our curls and made us "ooch" and wriggle. Then Dede gave us little smacks and called us boobies. The starch in the trimming about our knees was very scratchy. Dede snapped the white elastics under our chins as she put on our hats and said to Mother, "I wonder how long these youngsters will stay clean."

Being fixed up for the party was very painful.

There were three pairs of white cotton gloves waiting on the hall stand, like the mitts of the three little kittens. Mother sorted them and stroked them onto the fingers we held out as stiff as they'd go, and by the time that Mr. Russell's hansom cab, the only one in Victoria, jingled up to the door, we were quite ready.

Mother kissed us. Dede kissed us.

"Have you all got clean pocket handkerchiefs?"

Yes, we had.

"Don't forget to use them."

No, we wouldn't.

"Be sure to thank Miss Langley for the nice time."

"S'pose it isn't nice?"

"Say 'thank you' even more politely."

We sat in a row on the seat; Mr. Russell slammed the apron of the cab down in front of us, jumped up like a monkey to his perch at the back, and we were off—eight, six and four years old going to our first party.

It was such fun sitting there and being taken by the horse, just as if he knew all by himself where to find parties for little girls, for, after Mr. Russell had climbed up behind so that you could not see him, you forgot that there was a driver.

Lizzie looked over my hat and said to Alice, "I do hope this child will behave decently, don't you? There! See, already!" She pointed to the tips of my gloves which were all black from feeling the edge and buttons of the cab's inside.

"Stop it, bad child," she squealed so shrilly that a little door in the roof of the cab opened and Mr. Russell put his head in. When he saw it was only a "mad" squeal he took his head out again and shut up the hole.

We drove a long way before we came to the Langleys'. Their gate did not know which road it liked best, Moss or Fairfield, so it straddled the corner and gaped wide. We drove up to the door. The two Miss Langleys and Mr. Langley were there, shaking boys and girls by the hands.

The three Langleys had been grown-up a long, long time. They had big shining teeth which their lips hugged tight till smiles pushed them back and then you saw how strong and white the teeth were. They had yellow hair, blue eyes, and had to double down a long way to reach the children's hands.

Mr. Russell flung back the apron of his cab but we still kept on sitting there in a close row like the three monkeys, "See no evil, hear no evil, and speak no evil." He said, "Come now, little leddies. Me 'oss and 'ansom baint inwited." He lifted me out and Mr. Langley had to pull the others from the cab, for now that we were in the middle of the party Lizzie was as scared as any of us. She took Alice by one hand and me by the other and we shook hands with all the Langleys, for no matter how scared Lizzie was she always did, and made us do, what she knew was right.

The house was the wide, sitting sort. Vines and creepers tied it down to the ground.

The garden was big. It had trees, bushes and lawns— there were rocks covered with ivy, too.

The Langleys tried to mix the children by suggesting "hide and seek" among the bushes. Everybody hid but no one would seek. Each child wanted to hold a hand belonging to another of its own family. The boys were very, very shy and the girls' clothes so starchy they rattled if they moved.

By and by Miss Langley counted ... "Sixteen," she said. "That is all we have invited so we had better start." Something was coming up the drive. Lizzie thought it was our cab and that Miss Langley meant that it was time to be going home, so she took us up to Miss Langley to say what Mother had told us to, but it was not Mr. Russell at all. It was Mr. Winter's big picnic carriage, all shiny and new, the one he had got specially for taking children to parties and picnics. There seemed to be no end to the amount of children he could stuff into this carriage, but there was, because, when they put me in, there was not a crack of space left except the door handle, so I sat on that. The boys

61

were all up in the front seat, swarming over Mr. Winter like sparrows. Behind sat all the little girls—so still—so polite. Suddenly I had a thought and cried, "If this door busted open I'd fall out!"

"Millie, don't say 'busted'. It's horrible! Say 'bursted'." Lizzie's face was red with shame.

We went to Foul Bay and had games on the beach. After we had played a long time Lizzie was just as clean as when we left home, Alice was almost as clean, and I was all mussed up, but they were not having half such a good time as I.

We went back to the Langleys' house for tea. There were all sorts of sandwiches and there was cocoa and two kinds of cake—one just plain currant, the other a most beautiful cake with pink icing and jelly.

Lizzie and Alice sat across the table from me and were being frightfully polite, taking little nibbling bites like ladies, holding their cups with one hand, and never forgetting "thank you".

My mug was big, it took both my hands. Even then it was heavy and slopped. Miss Langley said, "Oh, your pretty frock!" and tied a bib round me and pulled the little neck hairs so hard that I could not help one or two squeaks . . . they weren't big, but Lizzie scowled and whispered to Alice. I was sure she said, "Bad, dirty little thing." I was just going to make a face at her when Miss Kate Langley came with the splendid pink cake. I had a piece of the currant kind on my plate. I was so afraid Miss Kate would see it and pass me—maybe she would never come back— that I stuffed the currant cake into both cheeks and held my hand up as the girls did at lessons if they wanted something.

"Jelly cake, dear?"

I couldn't speak, but I nodded. Lizzie's forehead crinkled like cream when mother was skimming for butter. She mouthed across at me, "I'm going to tell." My mouth was too busy to do anything with, but I did the worst I could at her with my eyes and nose. She had spoilt everything.

Somehow the jelly cake was not half as nice as I thought it was going to be.

The moment tea was over Miss Langley took my bib off and, holding me by the wrists with my hands in the air, said:

"Come, dear. Let me wash you before . . ."

She washed beautifully, and was a lovely lady. I told her about my cat Tibby, and after she had washed my face she kissed it.

I felt very special going back to the others with my hand in that of the biggest and best Miss Langley.

Out on the lawn they were playing "Presents for shies." Mr. Langley stuck up four wobbly poles and put a prize on top of each—bells and tops and whistles. If your shy hit a pole so that a prize fell off, it was yours to keep. I wanted a whistle most dreadfully. When my turn came my shy flew right over the other side of the garden. I had been quite sure that I could knock the whistle off the pole but my shy stick just would not do it. I had three tries and then I ran to Alice who was sitting on a bench and put my head down in her lap and howled. She lifted me by the ribbon and spread her handkerchief under my face so that I should not spoil her dress. Miss Langley heard my crying.

"There, there!" she said and gave me a little muslin bag with six candies in it—but it was not a whistle.

Lizzie told Miss Langley that she was very ashamed of me and that I always did behave dreadfully at parties. That made me stop crying and shout, "I never, never went to one before." Then I did make the very worst face I knew how at Lizzie and gave two sweets to Alice, two to Miss Langley, two to myself, and threw the empty bag at Lizzie as she went off to have her shy. I don't know how I should have felt if she had won a whistle but when she came back without any prize I picked up the bag and put the candy I was not eating in it and gave it to her.

Jingle, jingle, clop, clop—Mr. Russell's cab was coming up the drive. Again Lizzie marched us to Miss Langley.

"Thank you for a very nice party, Miss Langley," she said.

Then she poked at Alice, but Alice only went red as a geranium! She had forgotten what it was she had to say. Poor Lizzie looked down at me and saw the spot of jelly, the cocoa and the front part of me where I'd gone under the bush after my shy stick. She pushed me back and pulled her own clean skirt across me quickly.

When Lizzie wasn't looking at her Alice could remember all right. She said, "Miss Langley, I liked myself, and I'm glad I came."

Miss Langley gave her such a lovely smile that I tore my hand from Lizzie's, ran up and tiptoed, with my face as high as it would go, for Miss Langley to kiss.

We all jumped into the cab then and the apron slammed off everything but our heads and waving hands. The cab whisked round. The party was gone.

"Where're your gloves?"

"L—l—lost."

"Where's your hankie?"

"L—l—lost."

Lizzie took out her own and nearly twisted the nose off my face.

"I'm going to tell Mother about 'busted', about grabbing the jelly cake with your mouth full, about having to wear a bib and be washed. Oh! and there's the two lost things as well. I expect you'll get spanked, you disgusting child. I'm shamed right through about you, and I'm never, never, never going to take you to a party again."

One of my eyes cried for tiredness and the other because I was mad.

Alice got out her hankie, her very best one with Christmas scent on it. "Keep it," she whispered, pushing it into my hand. "Then there'll be only one lost thing instead of two."

British Columbia Nightingale

MY SISTER Alice was two years older than I and knew a lot. Lizzie was two years older than Alice and thought she knew it all. My great big sister *did* know everything. Mother knew all about God. Father knew all about the earth. I knew more than our baby, but I was always wondering and wondering.

Some wonders started inside you just like a stomach-ache. Some started in outside things when you saw, smelled, heard or felt them. The wonder tickled your thinking—coming from nowhere it got into your head running round and round inside until you asked a grown-up about this particular wonder and then it stopped bothering you.

Lizzie, Alice and I were playing in the garden when our Chinaboy Bong came down the path—that is how I know exactly what time of evening it was that this new noise set me wondering, because Bong was very punctual. The tassel on the end of his pigtail waggled all down the path and, as he turned out of the gate, it gave a special little flip. Then you knew that it was almost bed-time. It was just as the slip-slop of Bong's Chinese shoes faded away that I first noticed that new noise.

First it was just a little bunch of grating snaps following each other very quickly, as if someone were dragging a stick across a picket fence as he ran. The rattles got quicker and quicker, more and more, till it sounded as if millions of sticks were being dragged across millions of fences.

I said, "Listen girls! What is it?"

Alice said she did not hear anything in particular.

Lizzie said, "It's just Spring noises, silly!"

First the sound would seem here, then there, then everywhere—suddenly it would stop dead and then the stillness startled you, but soon the rattles would clatter together again filling the whole world with the most tremendous racket, all except just where you stood.

I was glad when my big sister put her head out of the window and called, "Bed-time, children!" I wanted to pull the covers up over my head and shut out the noise.

We went into the sitting-room to kiss Father and Mother goodnight. The fire and the lamp were lighted. Mother was sewing—Father looked at her over the top of his newspaper and said:

"Listen to British Columbia's nightingale, Mother! Spring has come."

Mother replied, "Yes, he certainly does love Spring in the Beacon Hill skunk-cabbage swamp!"

"Come along, children!" called Big Sister.

Upstairs our bedroom was full of the noise. It came pouring in through the dormer window. When the candle was taken away it seemed louder because of the dark. I called to Big Sister as she went down the stair, "Please may we have the window shut?"

"Certainly not! Stuffy little girl! The night is not cold."

"It isn't the cold, it's the noise."

"Noise? Fiddlesticks! Go to sleep."

I nosed close to Alice, "Do you know what nightingales are Alice?"

"Some sort of creature."

"They must be simply *enormous* to make such a big noise."

Alice's "uh-huh" was sleep talk.

I lay trying to "size" the nightingale by its noise. Our piano even with sister Edith pounding her hardest could never fill the whole night like that. Our cow was bigger than the piano, but even when they shut her calf away from her and great moos made her sides go in and out, her bellows only rumbled round the yard. This nightingale's voice crackled through the woods, the sky and everywhere. The band that played in the Queen's birthday parade died when you lost sight of it. This sound of something which you could not see at all filled the world. Why, even the cannon that went off at Esquimalt for people to set their watches by every night at nine-thirty and made Victoria's windows rattle, went silent after one great bang, but this monster in Beacon Hill Park adjoining our own property kept on and on with its roar of crackles.

I knew now why we were never allowed to go into Beacon Hill swamp to gather spring flowers: it was not on account of the mud at all, but because of this nightingale monster.

"I shall never, never go into Beacon Hill Park again," I said to myself. "I won't let on I'm scared but when we go for a walk I shall say, 'Let's go to the beach, it's much nicer than the Park.' "

I thought, "Perhaps she comes to the Park like the birds to nest in the Spring. Perhaps the Park might be safe in winter when the Monster went south."

I heard Father shoot the front-door bolt and the grown-ups coming up the stair. As the candles flickered past our door I whispered, "Mother!"

She came to me.

"Why are you not asleep?"

"Mother, how big is a nightingale?"

"Nightingales are small birds, we do not have them in Victoria."

Birds!—None in Victoria!

"But Father said—"

"That was just a joke, calling our little green frogs nightingales. Go to sleep, child."

Dear little hopping frogs!—I slept.

Time

FATHER was a stern straight man. Straight legs and shoulders; straight side-trim to his beard, the ends of which were straight-cut across his chest. From under heavy eyebrows his look was direct, though once in a rare while a little twinkle forced its way through. Then something was likely to happen.

Our family had to whiz around Father like a top round its peg.

It was Sunday. Father was carving the saddle of mutton. Everybody was helped. Father's plate had gone up for vegetables. Uncle and Auntie Hays were visiting us from San Francisco.

Father's twinkle ran up the table to Mother and zigzagged back, skipping Auntie, who was fixing her napkin over her large front with a diamond pin.

Father said, "What about a picnic on Saturday, Mother? We will have the omnibus and go to Mill Stream."

The two big sisters, we three little girls and the small brother were glad. Mother beamed on us all. Auntie attended to her mutton. Uncle never did have anything to say. He was like the long cushion in the church pew—made to be sat on.

All week we stared at the clock, but, for all she ticked, her hands stuck; it took ages for her to register even a minute. But Saturday did come at last and with it, sharp at ten, the yellow bus.

Uncle Hays made a nest of cushions in one corner of the bus for Auntie. Pies and cakes, white-wrapped and tucked into baskets like babies, the tea-billy wrapped in a newspaper petticoat—all were loaded in and we took our places and rattled away.

The bus had two horses and carpet seats. Its wheels were iron-bound and made a terrible racket over the stones.

Only the very middle of our town was paved and sprinkled; beyond the town was dust and bumps.

The seats of the bus were high. We three little girls discovered that we bumped less if we did not dangle, so we knelt on the seat and rested our arms on the open window ledges, till Auntie told Uncle he must shut all the windows except one, or the dust would ruin her new dust coat. After that we dangled and bumped.

Auntie grumbled all the way about Victoria's poor little blue water-barrel cart, that could only do the middle of the town, and told us of the splendid water-wagons of San Francisco.

At last we drove through a gate and down a lane and stopped. The driver opened the door and we all spilled out onto the grass beside a beautiful stream.

Uncle built a new nest for Auntie. There were pine boughs as well as pillows to it now, and she looked like a great fat bird sitting there peeping and cooing at Uncle over the edge.

The table-cloth was spread on the grass close to Auntie's nest. As soon as lunch was over Mother said, "Now children, run along. Don't go into the thick woods, keep by the stream."

Father looked at his watch and said, "It's now one o'clock —you have till five."

Downwards the stream broadened into a meadow; up-stream it bored a green tunnel through the forest, a tunnel crooked as a bed-spring. It curled round and round because there were so many boulders and trees and dams in the way.

The sides of the tunnel were forest, the top overhanging trees, the floor racing water.

We could not have squeezed into the woods had we tried because they were so thick, and we could not have seen where to put our feet, nor could we have seen over the top, because the undergrowth was so high.

Every twist the stream took it sang a different tune and kept different time. It would rush around the corner of a great boulder and pour bubbling into a still pool, lie there pretending it had come to be still, but all the time it was going round and round as if it was learning to write "O's"; then it would pour itself smoothly over a wedged log and go purling over the pebbles, quiet and dreamy. Suddenly it would rush for another turn, and roar into a rocky basin trickling out of that again into a wide singing place. It had to do all these queer things and use force and roughness to get by some of the obstacles. But sometimes the stream was very gentle, and its round stones were covered with a fine brown moss. When the moss was wet it looked just like babies' hair. You could pretend the stones were babies in their bath and the stream was sponging water over their heads.

Five-finger maidenhair ferns grew all along the banks. Some of them spread their thin black arms over the edge and, dipping their fingers in the water, washed them gently to and fro. Then the wind lifted them and tossed them in the air like thousands of waving hands. All kinds of mosses grew by the stream—tufty, flat, ferny, and curly, green, yellow and a whitish kind that was tipped with scarlet sealing wax.

Yellow eyes of musk blossoms peeped from crannies. They had a thick, soft smell. The smell of the earth was rich. The pines and the cedars smelled spicy. The wind mixed all the smells into a great, grand smell that made you love everything. There were immense sober pines whose tops you could not see, and little pines, fluffed out ready to dance. The drooping boughs of the cedars formed a thatch so thick and tight that creatures could shelter under it no matter how hard it rained. The bushes did not grow tight to the cedars because it was too dry and dark under them. Even their own lower limbs were red-brown and the earth bare underneath.

The wind sauntered up the stream bumping into everything. It was not strong enough to sweep boldly up the tunnel, but quivered along, giving bluffs and boulders playful little whacks before turning the next corner and crumbling the surface of that pool.

There was much to see as we went up the river, and we went slowly because there were so many things to get over and under. Sometimes there were little rims of muddy beach, pocked with the dent of deer hooves. Except for the stream the place was very quiet. It was like the stillness of a bird held in the hand with just its heart throbbing.

Sometimes a kingfisher screamed or a squirrel scolded and made you jump. I heard a plop down at my feet—it was a great golden-brown toad. I took him in my hands.

One sister said, "Ugh!" The other said, "Warts".

I put him in a tin and weighted it with a stone and hid it under a skunk cabbage.

We were very, very far up the stream, though it had not seemed a long way at all, when our big sister came around the bend behind us.

"Come children," she called. "It is time to go home."

We looked at each other. What did she mean? Time to go home? We had only just come.

I faced about.

"It is not," I said rudely, and received a smart box on the ear. But it was not our sister's word we doubted, it was Time.

I lagged behind to pick up the toad, wondering deeply about Time. What *was* Time anyway, that things could play such tricks with it? A stream could squeeze a whole afternoon into one minute. A clock could spread one week out into a whole year.

The baskets were packed. Uncle was building another nest for Auntie. Mother was seated in the bus looking very tired. Dick was asleep on the seat with his head in Mother's lap and his toy watch dangling out of his pocket.

I stared at the watch hard. The hands were at the same place they were when we started in the morning. Play things were always truer than real.

The bus started bumping along and the dust rolled behind. I sat opposite Auntie. I had draped a skunk cabbage leaf over the toad's tin.

"See dear, you will have to throw that leaf out of the window; the smell of it upsets Auntie." She detested me, and always tacked on that hypocritical "dear".

The leaf fluttered out of the window. I put my hand over the top of the tin.

"What have you got in the tin, dear? Let Auntie see."

I shot it under her nose, hoping it would scare her. It did. She gave a regular parrot-screech. The big sister reached across, seized the tin, looked, and flung tin, golden toad and all, out of the window.

Then suddenly those gone hours pulled out and out like taffy. It *was* late. The bus wheels started to roll quietly because we were in town now and under Mr. Redfern's big clock, which gave six slow sad strikes.

Father pulled out his big silver watch. Uncle pulled out a gold one. Auntie fussed with a fancy thing all wound up in lace and gold chains.

They all said "Correct", snapped the cases shut and put them back in their pockets.

I leaned against Father and shut my eyes.

Throb-throb-throb—was that Father's watch eating up minutes or was it hop-hop-hop, my golden toad, making his patient way down the long dusty road, back to the lovely stream where there was no time?

A LITTLE TOWN AND A LITTLE GIRL

Beginnings

VICTORIA, on Vancouver Island, British Columbia, was the
little town; I was the little girl.

It is hard to remember just when you first became aware
of being alive. It is like looking through rain onto a bald,
new lawn; as you watch, the brown is all pricked with pale
green. You did not see the points pierce, did not hear the
stab—there they are!

My father did not come straight from England to Victoria when, a lad of nineteen, he started out to see something of the world. He went to many countries, looking,
thinking, choosing. At last he heard of the California gold
rush and went there. He decided that California was a very
fine country, but after the rush was over he went back to
England, married an English girl and brought his bride
out to California in a sailing ship, all round Cape Horn. In-
tending to settle in California, he went into business but after
a while it irked Father to live under any flag other than
his own. In a few years, having decided to go back "home"
to live, he chartered a vessel and took to England the first
shipment of California wheat. But, staunch Englishman
though my Father was, the New Land had said something
to him and he chafed at the limitations of the Old which,
while he was away from it, had appeared perfect. His spirit
grew restless and, selling all his effects, he brought his wife
and two small daughters out to the new world. Round the
Horn they came again, and up, up, up the west coast of
America till they came to the most English-tasting bit of

all Canada—Victoria on the south end of Vancouver Island, which was then a Crown Colony.

Father stood still, torn by his loyalty to the Old Land and his delight in the New. He saw that nearly all the people in Victoria were English and smiled at how they tried to be more English than the English themselves, just to prove to themselves and the world how loyal they were being to the Old Land.

Father set his family down in British Columbia. He and Mother had accepted Canada long before I, the youngest but one of their nine children, was born. By that time their homesickness was healed. Instead of being English they had broadened out into being British, just as Fort Camosun had swelled herself from being a little Hudson's Bay Fort, inside a stockade with bastions at the corners, into being the little town of Victoria, and the capital of British Columbia.

Father bought ten acres of land—part of what was known as Beckley Farm. It was over James' Bay and I have heard my mother tell how she cried at the lonesomeness of going to live in a forest. Yet Father's land was only one mile out of the town. There was but one other house near—that of Mr. James Bissett of the Hudson's Bay Company. Mr. Bissett had a wife and family. They moved East long before I was born but I was to know, when nearly grown up, what the love of those pioneer women must have been for one another, for when years later I stood at Mrs. Bissett's door in Lachine, seeing her for the first time, and said, "Mrs. Bissett, I am Emily Carr's daughter, Emily," she took me to herself in the most terrific hug.

As far back as I can remember Father's place was all made and in order. The house was large and well-built, of California redwood, the garden prim and carefully tended. Everything about it was extremely English. It was as though Father had buried a tremendous homesickness in this new soil and it had rooted and sprung up English. There were hawthorn hedges, primrose banks, and cow pastures with shrubberies.

We had an orchard and a great tin-lined apple room, wonderful strawberry beds and raspberry and currant bushes, all from imported English stock, and an Isabella grape vine which Father took great pride in. We had chickens and cows and a pig, a grand vegetable garden—almost everything we ate grew on our own place.

Just one of Father's fields was left Canadian. It was a piece of land which he bought later when Canada had made Father and Mother love her, and at the end of fifty years we still called that piece of ground "the new field". The New Field had a snake fence around it, that is, a zigzag fence made of split cedar logs or of young sapling trees laid criss-cross, their own weight holding them in place so that they required no nails. Snake fences were extravagant in land and in wood, but wood and land were cheaper in Canada in early days than were nails and hinges. You made a gate wherever you wanted one by lowering bars to pass through and piling them up again. The only English thing in our new field was a stile built across the snake fence.

The New Field was full of tall fir trees with a few oaks. The underbrush had been cleared away and the ground was carpeted with our wild Canadian lilies, the most delicately lovely of all flowers—white with bent necks and brown eyes looking back into the earth. Their long, slender petals, rolled back from their drooping faces, pointed straight up at the sky, like millions of quivering white fingers. The leaves of the lilies were very shiny—green, mottled with brown, and their perfume like heaven and earth mixed.

James' Bay and Dallas Road

JAMES' BAY DISTRICT, where Father's property lay, was to the south of the town. When people said they were going over James' Bay they meant that they were going to cross a wooden bridge that straddled on piles across the James' Bay mud flats. At high tide the sea flooded under the bridge and covered the flats. It receded again as the tide went out with a lot of kissing and squelching at the mud around the bridge supports, and left a fearful smell behind it which annoyed the nose but was said to be healthy.

James' Bay was the part of the town to be first settled after Victoria had ceased to be a fort. Many Hudson's Bay men built fine homes across the Bay—Sir James Douglas, Mr. Alexander Munroe, Mr. James Bissett, Mr. James Lawson, Senator Macdonald, Bishop Cridge and Dr. Helmcken.

The district began at the south corner of the Bridge where Belville Street crossed it. Belville skirted the mud flats until they ended at Blanshard Street. On the other side of the Bridge, Belville ran along the harbour's edge, skipping places where it could not get to the water. When it came to the mouth of the harbour it met Dallas Road and doubled back along the shore of the Straits of Juan de Fuca, making a peninsula of the James' Bay District, the limit of which was Beacon Hill Park, a beautiful piece of wild land given to the people of Victoria by Sir James Douglas.

The Hill itself was grassy, with here and there little thickets of oak scrub and clumps of broom. Beyond the Hill the land was heavily wooded. When you climbed to the top of Beacon Hill and looked around you knew that the school geography was right after all and that the world really was round. Beacon Hill seemed to be the whole top of it and from all sides the land ran away from you and the edges were lost. To the west lay the purple hills of Sooke; to the south were the Straits of Juan de Fuca, rimmed by the snowy Olympic mountains, whose peaks were always playing in and out among the clouds till you could not tell which was peak and which sky. On the east there were more sea and islands. The town was on the north, with purple Cedar Hill and green Mount Tolmie standing behind it. Our winds came from the Olympics in summer and from the icy north in the winter.

There was a good race track measuring exactly one mile, running round the base of Beacon Hill. Here they had horse-racing and foot-racing. They played cricket and football on the flat ground outside the track, and there were sham battles between sailors and soldiers all over the Hill on the Queen's Birthday. In the woody swamps of the Park millions and millions of frogs croaked all through the Spring nights. They sounded as if all the world was made of stiff paper and was crackling up.

Dallas Road was the first pleasure drive made in Victoria. Everyone drove along it to admire the view. The road ran sometimes close to the edge of the clay cliffs and sometimes there were thickets of willow and wild rose bushes between. The trees and bushes were so waved by the beating of the wind that they grew crooked from always being pushed north when they were really trying to poke south into the sun. There were stretches of fine, soft grass on the cliffs and great patches of camass and buttercups. As the wind swept over these they looked as if they, too, were running away from the sea. How the petals of the wild roses managed to stick to their middles I can't think, but they did and the bushes were more pink than green in June. Their perfume, salted by the sea air, was the most wonderful thing that ever happened to your nose.

Beside one of the willow clumps on the Dallas Road were

two white picket fences, each just as long as a man. They were the graves of two sailors who died of smallpox before Victoria had a cemetery. The fences were kept painted but the names on the head-boards were faded right out.

Farther along Dallas Road on the two highest parts of the cliffs were set two cannons, hidden from the Straits by sodded earth mounds. These were really ammunition cellars, one on either side of each cannon; they had heavy-timbered and padlocked doors which we children longed to see inside. These cannons guarded the entrance to Esquimalt Harbour, a British naval base, three miles out from Victoria.

Most of the beaches below Dallas Road were pebbly and had rough, rocky points jutting out into the sea and dividing the long beaches and the little bays one from another. All the beaches were piled with driftwood—great logs bruised and battered out of all resemblance to trees except that some of them still had tremendous, interlocked roots tough as iron, which defied all the pounding of the waves, all the battering against the rocks to break them. The waves could only wash them naked and fling them high up on the beach to show man what he had to wrestle against under the soil of the Canadian West. But the settlers were not stopped. They went straight ahead taming the land. It took more than roots to stop those men.

The waters of the Straits were icy. Occasionally we were allowed to put on white cotton nightgowns and go bathing in the sea. Your body went down, the nightgown stayed up, icy cold bit through your skin. At the first plunge you had no breath left; when it came back it was in screeches that out-screamed the seagulls.

Silence and Pioneers

THE SILENCE of our Western forests was so profound that our ears could scarcely comprehend it. If you spoke your voice came back to you as your face is thrown back to you in a mirror. It seemed as if the forest were so full of silence that there was no room for sounds. The birds who lived there were birds of prey—eagles, hawks, owls. Had a song bird loosed his throat the others would have pounced. Sober-coloured, silent little birds were the first to follow settlers into the West. Gulls there had always been; they began with the sea and had always cried over it. The vast sky spaces above, hungry for noise, steadily lapped up their cries. The forest was different—she brooded over silence and secrecy.

When we were children Father and Mother occasionally drove out beyond the town to Saanich, Metchosin or the Highland District, to visit some settler or other carving a home for his family in the midst of overwhelming growth —rebellious, untutored land that challenged his every effort. The settler was raising a family who would carry on from generation to generation. As he and his wife toiled at the breaking and the clearing they thought, "We are taming this wilderness for our children. It will be easier for them than for us. They will only have to carry on."

They felled mighty trees with vigour and used blasting powder and sweat to dislodge the monster roots. The harder they worked with the land, the more they loved these rooty little brown patches among the overwhelming green. The pioneer walked round his new field, pointing with hardened, twisted fingers to this and that which he had accomplished while the woman wrestled with the inconveniences of her crude home, planning the smart, modern house her children would have by and by, but the children would never have that intense joy of creating from nothing which their parents had enjoyed; they would never understand the secret wrapped in virgin land.

Mr. Scaife, a pioneer, had digged a deep ditch round his forest field. The field was new ploughed. He showed Father with pride how few blackened stumps there were now left in the earth of it. I let go of Father's hand to gather wild flowers among the pokes of the snake fence. I fell into the deep, dry ditch. Brambles and tall grasses closed over my head, torn roots in the earthy sides of the ditch scraped me as I went down. It was the secret sort of place where snakes like to wriggle and where black hornets build their nests—nearly dark, only a little green light filtering through the brambles over my head. I screamed in terror. Willie Scaife, a farm lad, jumped into the ditch and pulled me out. He was my first hero.

The first Victorians could tell splendid stories of when Victoria was a Hudson's Bay Post, was called Fort Camosun and had a strong blockade about it with a bastion at each corner to protect the families of the Hudson's Bay men from Indians and wild beasts.

Though my parents did not come to Victoria till after the days of the Fort and I was not born for many years after that, still there were people in Victoria only middle-aged when I was little, who had lived in the old Fort and could actually tell you about it. Nothing delighted me more than to hear these "still-fresh-yesterday" stories, that were not old "once-upon-a-timers"! You could ask questions of the very story people themselves and they did not have to crinkle their foreheads, trying to remember a long way back.

There was a childless couple with whom I was a favourite —Mrs. Lewis and her husband, the sea captain. Mrs. Lewis had been Miss Mary Langford before her marriage. Her Father was Captain Langford, a naval man. I am not certain whether the Langfords ever actually lived in the Fort or not but they came to Victoria at the very beginning of its being. Captain Langford built a log farmhouse six or seven miles out from town. The district was named for him.

Sometimes when Captain Lewis was away Mrs. Lewis invited me to stay with her for company. They lived on Belville Street, on the same side of James' Bay as we did, in a pretty cottage with flowers and canaries all over it. The windows overlooked the Harbour and Mrs. Lewis could watch the Captain's boat, the old paddle-wheel steamer, *Princess Louise,* go and come through the Harbour's mouth, and could wave to the Captain on his bridge. It was Captain Lewis who took me for my first trip by sea, and later, when the Railway was built to Nanaimo, for my first trip by rail. When you put your hand in his it was like being led about by a geography (he knew everywhere) and Mrs. Lewis was history. Seated at her feet before the fire among the dogs and cats, I listened open-mouthed to tales of early Fort days.

Mrs. Lewis was a good teller. She was pretty to watch. The little bunch of black curls pinned high at the back of her head bobbed as she talked and her eyes sparkled. She told how young Naval officers used to take the pretty Miss Langfords out riding. When they came to Goldstream and Millstream, which were bubbling rivers with steep banks, that crossed the Langford trails, the men would blindfold the girls' horses and lead them across the river, using as a bridge a couple of fallen logs. One night as they were hurrying along a narrow deer trail, trying to get home before dark, they saw a panther stretched out on the limb of a tree under which they must pass in single file. The bushes were too dense for them to turn aside, so each rider whipped his horse and made a dash along the trail under the panther.

Mrs. Lewis told, too, of the coming of their piano from England. It sailed all round Cape Horn and was the first piano to come into the Colony of British Columbia. It landed at Esquimalt Harbour and was carried on the backs of Indians in relays of twenty at a time through a rough bush trail from Esquimalt to Langford. The tired Indians put the piano down in a field outside the house to rest a minute. The Langford girls rushed out with the key, unlocked and played the piano out there in the field. The Indians were very much astonished. They looked up into the sky and into the woods to see where the noise came from.

The stories jumped sharply out of Mrs. Lewis's mouth almost catching her breath, as she recalled vividly the excitement which these strange happenings had brought to her and to her sister, just out from their sheltered English life.

Sometimes Mrs. Cridge, Mrs. Mouat, Doctor Helmcken, or some of Sir James Douglas's daughters, all of whom had lived in the old Fort, would start chatting about old days and then we younger people would stand open-mouthed thinking it must have been grand to live those exciting experiences.

"It was, my dears," said Mrs. Cridge, "but remember too that there were lots of things to face, lots of things to do without, lots of hardships to go through."

I was a very small girl when the business men of Victoria chartered a steamer and, accompanied by their families, made a tour of Vancouver Island. It took the boat, the *Princess Louise,* ten days to go all round the Island. My Father and two of my sisters went. I was thought to be too small but I was not too small to drink in every word they said when they came back.

Father was overwhelmed by the terrific density of growth on the Island. Once when they were tied up for three hours he and another man took axes and tried to see how far they could penetrate into the woods in the given time. When the ship's whistle blew they were exhausted and dripping with sweat but their attack on the dense undergrowth scarcely showed. Father told of the magnificent trees, of their closeness to each other, of the strangling undergrowth, the great silence, the quantity of bald-headed eagles. "Really bald, Father?" I asked, but he said they were a rusty black all over except for white heads which shone out against the blue sky and the dark forest. Great white owls flew silently among the trees like ghosts, and, too, they had seen bears and whales.

One of my sisters was more interested in the passengers on the boat and made a lot of new friends. The other told me about the Indian villages where the boat had touched. This was all far more interesting to me than the stories people had to tell when they came back from trips to the Old Country, bragging about the great and venerable sights of the Old Land. I did not care much about old things. These wild, western things excited me tremendously. I did not long to go over to the Old World to see history, I wanted to see *now* what was out here in our West. I was glad Father and Mother had come as far as the West went before they stopped and settled down.

Saloons and Roadhouses

ON ALMOST every street corner in Victoria there was one saloon or more. There were saloons in the middle of every block as well.

I used to think that every saloon belonged to the Navy because sailors, wearing little boys' collars and wide trouser legs that flapped round their feet, rolled in and out of saloon doors at all times. These doors swung to noiselessly. They were only pinafore doors, made of slats and flapped to so quickly when a sailor went in or out that you never got a chance to see what it was they hid, not even if you were right in front when one was pushed open and nearly knocked you over. We were strictly forbidden to look at a saloon in passing. Grown-ups dragged you quickly past and told you to look up the street though there was nothing whatever to see there.

This made me long to know what was inside saloons. What was it that we were not supposed to see? Why was it naughty to twist your neck and look? You heard laughing and singing behind the swing doors. What did they do in there?

There were saloons, too, every few miles along the driving roads. These they called roadhouses. Each had two doors. Over one was written "Parlour", over the other, "Bar". These roadhouses were most attractive; they had verandahs with beautiful flower-boxes at the windows, filled with gay flowers and drooping, five-finger maidenhair fern. Very often they had cages of birds and of wild animals too. The Colonist Hotel in Beacon Hill Park had a panther on its verandah. The Four Mile House had a cage of raccoons. Another roadhouse had a baby bear and another a cage of owls.

Once when Aunt and Uncle were visiting us from San Francisco we took a long drive on a hot day. When we got to the top of the Four Mile Hill Uncle poked Father. Father ignored the poke and we passed the bar and drove to the bottom of the hill. Then Father dug the driver in the back and he pulled up his horses. Father, Uncle and the driver all toiled up the hill again on foot, leaving us sitting in the hack by the roadside. We children were allowed to get out and gather wild roses. I slipped behind the hack and started up the hill to have a look at the coons in the cage. Mother called me back. Auntie said something about "the unwholesome nosiness of little people".

I said, "I just wanted to see the little coons, Auntie."

"Pick some roses for Auntie," she ordered, but when I did she threw them over the wheel. She said the dust on them made her sneeze.

Goodacre, the butcher, had a slaughter-house out on Cadboro Bay Road. Cattle and sheep were brought from the Mainland by boat and landed at the wharf in front of Father's store. They were then driven straight through the centre of the town, up Fort Street which, after it had gone straight in the town, wiggled and twisted and called itself "Cadboro Bay Road".

The wild range cattle were crazed with fright. They bellowed and plunged all over the sidewalk, hoofing up the yellow dust. Women ran to shut their gates before the cattle rushed in and trampled their gardens. All the way up the street doors banged and gates slammed as everyone hurried to shelter.

I had been to visit my sister who lived on Fort Street. I was to go home by myself as there was no one to fetch me that day. It was the first time I had been through town alone. When I was just opposite the Bee Hive Saloon a drove of these wild cattle came tearing up the street. They were almost on top of me before I knew what all the dust and shouting and bellowing was about. Men with long whips whooped, dogs barked, the street seemed to be waving up and down with the dull red movement of beasts' backs bumping through the dust. Suddenly I was snatched up in a pair of huge black arms, a black face was near mine. It had grinning white teeth. We backed through the swing door and I was inside a saloon at last. The big black man set me down on the bar. The barkeeper and the negro ran to the window to look over the painted green glass at the boiling tumult of cattle outside. I could only hear their bellowing and scuttling.

I looked around the Saloon. Shiny taps were beside me and behind the long counter-bar ran shelves full of bottles and sparkling glasses; behind them again was looking-glass so that there seemed to be twice as many bottles and twice as many glasses as there really were, and two barmen and two negroes and two me's! In the back half of the saloon were barrels and small wooden tables; chairs with round backs stood about the floor with their legs sunk in sawdust; bright brass spitoons were everywhere. The saloon was full of the smell of beer and of sawdust. There was nothing else, nothing that I could see to make anyone sing.

The noise moved on up the street. The two men returned to the bar. The barman poured something yellow into a glass and shoved it towards the negro who threw back his head and gulped it like medicine. Then he lifted me down, held the swing door open and I went out into the still unsettled, choking dust of Fort Street.

My big sister had a kind heart. Nothing pleased her more than to drive old, lame or tired people into the country. There was always some ailing person tucked up in her little phaeton being aired. All about Victoria were lovely drives —Admiral Road, Burnside, Cadboro Bay, Cedar Hill. The country roads were very dusty and dry, so every few miles there was a roadhouse with a bar for men and a watering trough for horses—ladies went thirsty. No lady could possibly be seen going into a bar even if only for a glass of water.

We bought a new horse called Benny. His former master had been accustomed to look in at every roadhouse bar. Benny knew them every one. If my sister were talking to her invalid passenger and not noticing, Benny swerved gently up to the bar door and stopped so dead it unsettled the ladies' bonnets.

When my sister saw where she was she would give Benny a cut with the whip which would send him dashing from the saloon at a guilty gallop, my sister sitting very red and crooked behind him. She was sure just then to meet someone whom she knew and be too upset to bow and then she had double shame.

Ways of Getting Round

BEYOND the few blocks of Victoria upon which the shops stood the roads were of dirt and had sidewalks of one, two or three planks according to the street's importance. A great many people kept cows to supply their own families with milk. When their own pasture field was eaten down they turned the cow into the street to browse on roadside grass along the edges of the open ditches, or to meander out to the grassy land on top of the cliffs off Dallas Road. Victoria cows preferred to walk on the plank sidewalks in winter rather than dirty their hooves in the mud by the roadside. They liked to tune their chews to the tap, tap, tap of their feet on the planks. Ladies challenged the right of way by opening and shutting their umbrellas in the cows' faces and shooing, but the cows only chewed harder and stood still. It was the woman-lady, not the lady-cow who had to take to the mud and get scratched by the wild rose bushes that grew between sidewalk and fence while she excursioned round the cow.

If people did not wish their flowers to be turned into milk it was up to them to fence their gardens. Father's property was very securely fenced and his cows were always kept within their own pastures. We had a painted fence in front of our property, tarred fences on the sides, and our field had a snake fence.

There was no way to get about young Victoria except on legs—either your own or a horse's. Those people who had a field, a barn, and a cow usually kept a horse too.

The horses did not roam; they had to be kept handy for hitching. All the vehicles used were very English. Families with young children preferred a chaise, in which two people faced the horse and two the driver. These chaises were low and so heavy that the horse dragged, despondent and slow. The iron tires made such a rumbling over the rough stony roads that it was difficult to hear conversation while travelling in a chaise especially when to the rumble was added the rattle of wheel spokes that had got over-dry and loosened. What you did then was to drive as deep as you dared into the first stream you knew of and let the chaise wheels soak, all the while encouraging the horse to go forward and back, turning the wheels in the water until they swelled again. You could not go into very deep water for fear of drowning the driver for the chaises were set so low that the driver sat right down among the wheel hubs. If children fell out of these low chaises they did not get hurt, only dusty. The horse stood so much higher than the driver that there was a tall iron rack in the front to hold the reins so that the horse could not swish his tail over them and pin the reins down so tight that he could not be guided.

Men preferred to drive in high, two-wheeled dogcarts in which passengers sat back to back and bumped each other's shoulder blades. The seat of the driver was two cushions higher than that of the other passengers. Men felt frightfully high and fine, perched up there cracking the whip over the horse's back and looking over the tops of their wives' hats. There were American buggies, too, with or without hoods which could be folded back like the top of a baby's pram.

In Victoria nobody was in a particular hurry to get any-where—driving was done mostly for the pleasure of fresh air and scenery.

In town there were lots of livery stables where you could hire horses or could board your own. The smell of horse manure was so much a part of every street that it sat on your nose as comfortably as a pair of spectacles. Of course there were no livery stables among the drygoods, food, and chemists' shops. Everywhere else you saw "Livery Stable" printed above wide, cool entries and heard horses chewing and stamping, and saw long rows of tails swishing out of stalls on either side of a plankway while ugly, square vehicles called hacks stood handy waiting for horses to be hitched to them. These hacks for hire were very stuffy. The town had one imported hansom-cab which thought itself very smart, and there was Mr. Winter's picnic carriage, a huge vehicle that held as many children as the Old Woman's Shoe. When its wide, circular back seat was crammed and more children were heaped on top of Mr. Winter up on his high driver's seat, and they were all yelling, and yellow dust rolling, and wheels rumbling, it looked and sounded like a beehive swarming. For immense affairs like Sunday School picnics and excursions there were yellow buses with long rows of windows, long wooden seats, uncushioned except for strips of carpet running from driver to door. They had no springs to speak of, and were so noisy that you could not hear your own groans being bumped out of you.

Victoria's baker and butcher boys delivered meat and bread on horse-back, carrying their loaves and joints in huge wicker baskets rested against their hips. As soon as they had one foot in the stirrup and while their other leg was still flying in the air over the horse as he galloped off, they shouted "Giddap!" It was a wonder the boys did not grow crooked balancing such heavy baskets on their hips, but they did not—they were straight and strong. I used to wish I were a delivery boy to throw my leg across a horse and shout "Giddap!" to feel myself rush through the air, but I should have preferred bread to meat in my basket.

The first time I knew that Victoria was slower than other towns was when, at the age of twelve, I was recovering from typhoid fever and a lady whom Mother knew, and whose two children had had typhoid in the same epidemic as I, took me along with her little girls for a trip to Puget Sound.

It was my first visit to an American city and I felt giddy in the head from its rush. I heard Americans laugh and say "slow as Canadian" and call my town "sleepy old Victoria".

I heard one man say to another, "Went across the line this summer."

"Did eh? What sort of a place is Victoria?"

"Sleepiest ever!" laughed the first, "Every place of business had a notice up, 'Gone to lunch. Back in a couple of hours.' "

That was the first time I knew we were slow.

San Francisco was the biggest, the most important city on the Pacific Coast. It was a terrible trip in the small, bouncy steamer, down the rough coast. Victorians only went for something very, very important like a big operation or a complete change for health, to save their lives. Even then they stuck their noses up and said, "I am going across the line," or "going to the other side", as if the "other side" was an underneath and inferior side of the earth. But, if they had to have such an enormous operation that it was quite beyond Victoria's skill, then, rather than go all round the Horn back to England and either die before they got there or else get well and forget what the operation was for, they allowed San Francisco to "operate" them.

Americans dashed across the line sometimes to look at us Canadians and at British Columbia as if we had been dust-covered antiques. They thought English and Canadian people as slow and stupid as we thought the American people uncomfortable rushers—makers of jerry-built goods that fell to pieces in no time. We preferred to wait ages for our things to come by sailing ship round the Horn from England rather than to buy American goods. This annoyed the American manufacturers.

An aunt of ours in San Francisco sent us American dolls. They were much prettier than English dolls. The first that came were made of wax but they melted when we left them in the sun. Next Christmas she sent us bisque dolls, very lovely but too breakable to hug; we could not even kiss them but they cracked. We went back to our lovable old wood and china dolls that took their time to come to us all round the Horn, and, even if they were plain, they were substantial and could bear all the loving we gave them.

Father's Store

VICTORIA was like a lying-down cow, chewing. She had made one enormous effort of upheaval. She had hoisted herself from a Hudson's Bay Fort into a little town and there she paused, chewing the cud of imported fodder, afraid to crop the pastures of the new world for fear she might lose the good flavour of the old to which she was so deeply loyal. Her jaws went rolling on and on, long after there was nothing left to chew.

Government Street was the main street of the town. Fort Street crossed it and at the cross, in a little clump, stood most of the shops. On Yates, View and Broad Streets were a few lesser shops, several livery stables and a great many saloons. On Bastion Street stood the Courthouse and the Jail. Down on Wharf Street, facing the Harbour, were the wholesale houses. Fisgard, Cormorant and Johnson Streets were Chinatown. At the tail ends of all these streets were dwelling-houses set in gardens where people grew their own flowers and vegetables.

The rest of Victoria was higgledy-piggledy. It was the cows who laid out the town, at least that portion of it lying beyond the few main streets. Cow hooves hardened the mud into twisty lanes in their meanderings to and fro—people just followed in the cows' footsteps.

When the first settlers cut up their acreage, the resulting lots were all shapes and sizes. Owners made streets and lanes over the property anywhere that seemed convenient at the moment.

My father was a wholesale importer of provisions, wines

and cigars. His store was down on Wharf Street among other wholesale places. The part of Wharf Street where Father's store stood had only one side. In front of the store was a great hole where the bank of the shoreline had been dug out to build wharves and sheds. You could look over the top of these to the Songhees Indian Reserve on the opposite side of the Harbour. To one side of the hole stood the Hudson's Bay Company's store—a long, low building of red brick with a verandah. The Indians came across the Harbour in their dugout canoes to trade at the store. They squatted on the verandah, discussing new-bought goods, or their bare feet pattered up and down the board walks of Wharf Street. They were dressed in gay print dresses, plaid shawls and bright head handkerchiefs. Once I saw Father's man take out case after case of beautiful cluster Malaga raisins and pour them into the outspread shawls and hand-kerchiefs of the jabbering Indians, who held out their hands and stuffed their mouths, giving grunts of delight.

I asked Father. "Why do you give all these raisins to the Indians?"

He replied, "They are maggoty, the whole lot of them—but Indians love raisins and don't mind maggots at all."

At the opposite side of the Wharf Street hole stood the Customs House, close to the water's edge. Made of red brick, it was three storeys high and quite square. The Customs House steps were very dignified—high and wide-spread at the bottom. Underneath the steps was the Gregorys' door.

Gregory was an Old Country gardener. His wife was very homesick as well as really ill. The Gregorys were the caretakers of the Customs House. In front of their rooms they had a beautiful little garden, sheltered by a brick wall. Sometimes Mother sent Mrs. Gregory things and Mrs. Gregory gave us beautiful posies of flowers in exchange. On the lower floor of the Customs House, where the Gregorys had their quarters, there was a wide hall which ran straight through the building. The wind roared down this passage from a great doorway opening onto the Harbour. Furious

that the Gregorys' door under the steps was not big enough
to let it all out at once, it pounded and bellowed at all the
doors down the hall as it passed them. The waves came
dashing up the slip and rushed through the door and into
the hall. I used to think that ships sailed right into the
Gregorys' hall-way to do their customs business and I begged
to go to see Mrs. Gregory on any excuse whatever, always
hoping to meet a ship sailing down the hall-way. I was much
disappointed that I never struck a tide high enough to bring
a ship in. Once I thought I was going to but when no more
than two waves had washed in through the great doors
Mr. Gregory rushed out, shut and barred them.

The inside of Father's store was deep and dark. Cases,
crates, and barrels stood piled one on top of another right
up to the ceiling, with just a narrow lane running down
the middle and ending in what was called "the yard"—
not a yard at all, only a strong, rough board shed filled
with "empties" and cats. There were no windows; the cats
crawled in and out of the "empties" hunting for rats, their
eyes shining in the black. Slits of daylight cut between
the boards of the shed walls, and shadows thrown by a
sputtering gas jet made it all spooky and unreal—different
from the solid, comfortable feel of the outer store crammed
with provisions.

Father had every colour of cat. He took fresh milk in
a bottle from home every morning to them; he said a diet
of straight rat was not healthy for cats. Only one of them
was a comfortable, particular cat and came to sit by the
stove in Father's office. The rest were just wholesale cats.

Father's office was beside the open front of his big store
and in it Father sat in front of a large, square table covered
with green baize; on it in front of him was a cupboard full
of drawers and pigeon-holes. He sat in a high-backed wicker
armchair. His beard was white and, after he went bald,
he wore a black skull cap. A fat round stove, nearly always
red hot, was between Father's table and the long, high desk
where his men stood or sat on high stools doing their books
when they were not trundling boxes on a truck. There was

an iron safe in one corner of the office with a letter press on top and there were two yellow chairs for customers to sit on while Father wrote their orders in his book. Everything was dozened in Father's store: his was not a business that sold things by pinches in paper bags. High along the wall ran four long shelves holding glass jars of sample English sweets—all pure, all wholesome, all English. The labels said so.

New Neighbours

AS I FIRST remember it, James' Bay district had many fields and plenty of wooded land left, but houses began to creep nearer and nearer to ours and the fields were being cut up into town lots. I was very sorry when Bishop Cridge's big, wild field opposite us was sold. The Bishop's house sat back in the little bit of wood with an orchard and two fields. His driveway curved and had laurels and little bushes of yellow roses all the way up. We children used to play "ladies" in the Bishop's wild field with his three little girls. Being the youngest of the six children I could never be a "lady"—I had always to be "bad child", while the play mothers fed me on green gooseberries, wild and very sour.

The Bishop's house was built some time after Father's. The street was very narrow and in that one long block from Toronto to Simcoe Street there was only his house and ours. Father gave a good strip of his land to make the street wider; so the City named it Carr Street after Father. Carr Street would have joined Birdcage Walk if Mrs. McConnell's cow farm had not stood in the way, and Birdcage Walk would have been Government Street if the James' Bay Bridge had not been there to get people over the mud flats. After many years Government Street swallowed them up—James' Bay Bridge, Carr Street and Birdcage Walk—and went straight out to Dallas Road.

One day when we were playing "ladies" in the Bishop's field and I, the "baby", was being hidden in the bushes from the ferocious wild beast which ate children but which was really the Bishop's gentle cow "Colie", some men climbed over the fence. They had instruments on three legs which they set beside the road and squinted through. They came right into our mock-orange parlour and our gooseberry-bush dining-room. They swept the tin cans which had furnished our kitchen from our own particular log and sat down upon it and wrote in little books. They even tore pickets off the fence. The cow was taken to another enclosure, wagons dumped lumber and bricks all over the field. Soon real houses stood on top of our pretend ones, real ladies smacked real babies and pushed prams right on top of where our fun had been, and Mother was sending us across to ask if the new neighbour would like pots of tea or anything till her own stove was up.

Visiting Matrons

VICTORIA matrons did not fritter away their time in the paying of short calls. They had large families. The Chinese help could not be left in charge of the nursery while the mothers went visiting. So when they came to call, they brought their family along and stayed. Besides, unless people had a horse, there was no way of getting about other than on foot. So ladies took their families of young children along, packing the baby into the pram, wedging him in firmly with feeding bottles, infant necessities, a bag of needlework and the mother's little lace cap in a paper bag. After an early lunch they started immediately, prepared to make a day of it. The visit had been planned between the two ladies a long time ahead, weather permitting.

Average ladies had six children. When a family visited us the eldest wheeled the youngest in the pram. They all trooped through our gate. First the baby was exhibited, fed and put to sleep. Then the visitor took off her bonnet and put on her cap. The children dispersed to see dolls, pets and eat enormous quantities of fruit picked right off the trees. Our visitors were always very anxious about their families when they heard of all the plums, apples, cherries and pears they had eaten while the ladies sat sewing in the garden. Mother told them not to worry and none of them ever died of it. Mother knew a certain number of families whom she invited to our garden for one long summer afternoon every year.

My big sister used to visit a friend who had three little

girls the same ages as we three. We played with them while the ladies visited in the drawing-room.

Those children had all the things we did not, and we had what they did not. They lived on the waters of the Arm and had a boat. They had a pony and a big kennel of hunting dogs. Their Mama was stern and their Papa easy; *our* Father was stern, our Mother easy. Our garden was prim and theirs rambling.

Those friends were as far from town on the other side as we were from town on our side. There were two bridges to cross and ever so many different kinds of smells to pass through. From our own gate to the James' Bay Bridge wild rose bushes grew at the roadsides nearly all the way and their perfume was delicious. Then we came to the mud flats and our noses hurt with its dreadfulness when the tide was out. We had no sooner got over that than there was China-town with stuffy, foreign smells. Then came the gas-works —this smell was said to be healthful but it was not nice. Rock Bay Bridge had more low-tide smells, which were made easier by a sawmill; the new sawdust smelled so nice that you forgot your nose until the other end of the bridge came. There sat a tannery from which came, I thought, the worst smell of them all. There was one still more dreadful—Parker's slaughter-house and piggery—but that was two miles further on and we did not have to pass it on the way to call on our friends.

Sometimes our friends rowed us down to James' Bay Bridge in their boat and we slipped past all the smells and were home in no time.

In early Victoria there were family evening parties to which the father, mother and all sizes of growing children went together and at which they played charades, dumb crambo, guessing games and forfeits. There was music, too, for nearly everyone could play at least one piece on the piano or sing a song or do a recitation, or they did things together. Nobody minded if it was not quite perfect. Every-one laughed just the same. Everyone helped to entertain the others and you did some trick or told a story if you could not sing. My two big sisters went to Navy balls occasionally, but Father did not approve of the way Victoria mothers scrambled among the Navy to find husbands for their daughters. He was very strict; he had made a nice home for us and thought we should stay in it.

Another form of young Victoria entertainment was the church conversazione. The Bishop opened, shut and blessed the affair but the congregation did the talking. Conversaziones were held in the church schoolroom which the ladies cut into little cubicles with benches—three sitting sides and one open. The benches were just close enough for one lady's lips to reach across confidentially to the opposite lady's ear. There was music for people who were not chatty and when everything had been done and encored tea was served. Young girls carried it to the cubicles. Both sexes and all ages came to conversaziones. You had to pay only two bits, which was twenty-five cents, for all the talking, listening, music, tea and the Bishop's blessing.

Presbyterians had what were called church socials but, as they were held in the church itself, personal conversation was very restricted. Dr. Reid told stories from the pulpit, there was choir singing and no tea.

As Victoria grew bigger, social groups grew smaller, selecting only those people who were congenial to each other. They became too a great deal more particular about the ability of performers and the quality of entertainment. Victoria stood like a gawky girl, waiting, waiting to be a grown-up city.

Servants

WHAT WITH big families and only green little Chinese boys for servants, Victoria matrons were kept busy. The boys came from China at the age of twelve. It took much patience to teach these foreign children our language as well as how to work.

English servants who came out to Canada did so with the firm determination of finding a husband in a hurry and of making homes and raising families who would be not servants but masters. While waiting for the husbands these women accepted positions, grumbling from morning till night at the inconveniences of the West. There were hosts of bachelors trying to make good in this new world—men who were only too willing to marry a helpmate. Love did not much matter if she was competent and these women in their turn were glad enough to go through drudgery and hardship if they were working for themselves and for their own independence. Man and wife each got something from the bargain and pushed forward, keeping step choppily, getting used to each other's gait. While these imported-from-England domestics were creating a class to put themselves into, Victoria ladies made do with raw, neat pigtailed, homesick China boys. Many a muddly housewife, accustomed to good servants in the Old Country, had first herself to learn how to run a house before she could teach her Chinese help.

The Chinese all wore clothes cut from exactly the same pattern—long black pants, loose white shirts worn outside the pants, white socks and aprons, cloth shoes with soles an inch thick and no heels. They scuffed along with a little dragging slip-slop sound.

The Chinese kept themselves entirely to themselves like rain drops rolling down new paint—learning our ways, keeping their own. When their work was done they put on black cloth coats made the same shape as their white shirts, let the pigtail which had been wound round their heads all day drop down their backs, and off they went to Chinatown to be completely Chinese till the next morning. They learned just enough of our Canadian ways to earn Canadian money —no more.

Our Chinaboy, Bong, was not pretty—he was pock-marked; but Bong was a good boy and was part of our child-hood. He came to Mother at the age of twelve, green and homesick, without one word of English. When things were more than Bong could bear he sat down and cried. Then Mother patted his shoulder as if he had been one of her own children and said, "Come on, Bong, be a good boy," and Bong would rub his big sleeve across his eyes, run out to the barn and sing a little Chinese song to the cow. The cow was a great comfort to Bong. She would stop chewing, roll back her ears and listen to the Chinese words as if she understood them. Bong loved her.

Bong stayed with us for many years. We were all as fond of him as one could be of anything holding itself so com-pletely aloof. He seemed really to love my little brother. When Bong went back to China to see his mother, he left a hole in our kitchen and a hole in the cow yard, queer, foreign holes, belonging and not belonging to us, for Bong never had become one bit Canadian in all the years he worked for us in Canada.

There was Wash Mary too, an Indian woman who came to wash for Mother every Monday. She was gentle, had a crinkled-up skin and was so small she had to stand on a block to reach her washtub. The Indian in Mary was more human and understandable than the Chinese in Bong.

The wash-house was across the yard. First Mary lit the stove; then she hung her shawl up on a nail and there was her thin, lumpy little body, buttoned into a pink print dress with a very full skirt reaching right to her bare feet. But her clothes were western, not eastern like Bong's. She took off the black silk handkerchief that bound her head. Her hair, thick and black, stood up from both sides of the parting that began at her forehead and ended at the back of her neck. On each side the hair was roped into a thick plait. The right plait had nothing to do with the left till after it had reached and rested on her shoulder blades; then the plaits were united again, tied together with a bit of string and looped across Mary's shoulders like a strong, splendid handle.

Mary was a wonderful washer. The suds boiled up to her shoulders and the steam about her faded the wrinkles till she looked almost young. Up and down, up and down, she went over her washboard, her brown eyes staring and her mouth tied up in puckers. It was a big mouth that could hold six clothes pins at once. After our lines were full of washing and Mother's clothes white as snow, and after Mary had enjoyed a good dinner in our kitchen, she shut herself into the wash-house and washed and dried all the clothes she wore, drying them quickly over the fire. Then she knotted her dollar into the corner of her new-washed handkerchief and went smiling out of the gate.

Mary was not a Songhees Indian. She lived in a little house in Fairfield.

East and West

CHINAMAN and Indian played a very real part in young Victoria.

The Chinaman shuffled along in heelless shoes with his vegetable or fish baskets swinging. He peddled his wares with few words. The Indian's naked feet fell pat-pat upon the earth roads. It was the Chinese man but the Indian woman who shouldered the burden. The Chinaman's wife was back home in China. The Indian rolled leisurely and with empty hands, behind his squaw. A cedar-root burden basket of her own weaving was slung across the woman's back, steadied by a woven pack strap worn across the chest. Women of some tribes wore the strap across their foreheads, pushing their heads forward against the burden's weight.

The Indian squatted upon each doorstep to rest. The Chinaman never rested—he kept up his mechanical jog-trot all day. He lived frugally, sending the earnings of his brown, calloused hands and his sweating toil home to China. The Indian wasted no sweat on labour—he took from nature those things which came easiest. What money he earned he spent in the nearest store immediately, exchanging it for whatever pleased his eye or his stomach. The Indian's money circulated; he had no idea of its value nor of saving it. The satisfying of immediate needs was enough for him. To our sombre landscape his careless picturesqueness was an enrichment. He was the link between the primitive and civilization. Unlike the Chinese vegetable gardener who forced the land to produce so that he might make money from it, money to send back to China, taking the land's goodness, not caring to put anything back, the native Indian sat staring, enjoying leaving Nature to do her own work while he got along with a minimum of exertion and a great deal of happiness.

The white man more or less understood the childlike Indian; he belonged to his own hemisphere. The Oriental eluded him.

A Cup of Tea

ONE NIGHT an Indian family beached their canoe on the shore below Cook Street. Indians were allowed to pitch a tent and remain the night on any beach during their long canoe journeys up and down the Coast.

This party of Indians was coming to Victoria but there was no hurry, the waves were high and night came down. The canoe contained the family and all they owned. There was a man, a woman, three children, one dog, two cats, a crate of fowls, besides a tent, bedding, cooking utensils, fishing gear, clothes and odd bits of hoarded possessions gleaned from Nature's bounty or from man's discards.

They flung an old tent across a conveniently low willow bough that stuck out of the bank. The unpegged sides of the tent flapped and billowed in the wind, rain drizzled. They tossed the bedding under the tent. The man, dog and cats crept at once into its cosiness.

The woman and children huddled round a low beach fire, tending the black iron cooking-pot and the tall tin for the brewing of tea. A sleeping child was tucked among the shapeless folds of the woman's motherliness, under her shawl. The movement of her arms across his sleeping body did not disturb him when she mended the fire. She was tired with his heaviness and from the sweep of her paddle all day long. She yawned, lolled back against a log and swept the bay with eyes used to judging what wind and waves were up to. Suddenly she called to her man; a lazy hand raised the canvas. The man followed with screwed-up eyes the woman's pointing finger.

Out in the bay a lone Chinaman in a clumsy fish-boat was wrestling with his sail. The unwieldy craft lay over first to one side, then to the other, her sail almost flat to the water. That the man in her did not tip out was a marvel.

The Indian man and woman left their fire and their supper. Waddling across the pebbles, they launched the heavy canoe. The woman laid her baby in the bow, close under the canoe's wolf-head prow, while she did a full share of the shoving and grunting necessary to launch the craft. It was she who stepped into the icy water to give the final freeing push, then she got into the canoe which was already staggering among the waves. She took her steering paddle and directed the canoe how to cut each wave. The man doggedly dipped, dipped, dipped his paddle, giving force, but not guidance.

They helped the Chinaman to ship his sail and clamber into their canoe. They brought him ashore, towing his boat behind them.

The Chinaman's face was a greenish mask; nervous grins of gratitude were strewn over it. He sat himself uncomfortably on a log near the Indians' fire. They squatted round their fish pot, dog and cats skulked near, hoping. The man dipped, the woman and the children dipped. The Chinaman dipped but, too embarrassed, ate sparingly. No words were spoken. The only sound was that of clams being sucked from their shell and the brittle rap of the empties flung among the stones.

The woman poured tea into a tin cup and passed it to the Chinaman. The sham grin left the man's face, his Oriental mask dropped. Bowing to the woman, he raised the steaming liquid to his lips, made a kissing sound into the tea and sluiced its warmth noisily into every corner of his mouth before the great gulps gurgled down his throat. The woman nodded.

"Uh-huh!" she said, and smiled.

Cathedral

CHRIST CHURCH CATHEDRAL sat on the top of Church Hill. The Hill sloped gently to the town on its north side and sharply down to James' Bay on the south, with shelves and sheer drops where rock had been blasted out for road-making.

A French family by the name of Jourand built Rocca-bella, a large boarding-house on the south side of Church Hill just below the Cathedral. It had a beautiful garden and was a quietly superior place in which to stay, holding its own even after modern conveniences in other boarding-houses overtook its level, clinging to its little open fire-places and defying central heating. English guests particularly favoured Roccabella. They liked the sound of the Cathedral bells that came quavering in through their windows. They liked to sit by their own particular fire and to look across James' Bay to the snowy Olympics.

The first Cathedral was burned down. The one I remember was built of wood and had a square tower with a cross on top. As Victoria grew they kept adding wings and more wings to the Cathedral till it looked squat and mother-hennish. Brick and stone churches sprang up in other parts of the city but the national significance of the old wooden Cathedral, sitting on the top of its hill, made it, in comparison with the others, like the star on top of a Christmas tree. The tree's other ornaments seemed mere baubles. Christ Church Cathedral was the emblem of our National Faith. It meant something to every Briton, whether he realized it or not, whether he were Methodist,

Presbyterian, Roman Catholic, no matter what he worshipped, even if he professed no religion at all. There was something particularly British, something secure about it.

Our family did not attend Christ Church Cathedral. Mother went to the Reformed Episcopal Church on Humboldt Street. Church Hill was too steep for her to climb and anyways she liked the evangelical service.

Bishop Cridge of the Reformed Episcopal Church had once been Dean of the Cathedral, but, long before I can remember, he and Bishop Hills had had a bitter clash of conscience—"High" and "Low", that same old controversy that never will be settled while people are people. Spiteful folks spoke of this church split as "the Big Church kicking the Little Church down the hill." The little church smiled up from the mud flats, the Cathedral frowned down, austere and national, and Victorians chose High or Low, whichever comforted them most.

Cemetery

THE FIRST cemetery that I can remember was on Quadra Street. It was only one-half block big and was already nearly full when we went through it coming from church one Sunday morning. It had a picket fence and was surrounded by tall, pale trees whose leaves had silver backs. Except for what care relatives gave the graves, it was a wild place, grave being tied to grave by a network of brambles and vines. There were one or two handsome headstones among the mat of wild and tame, flowers and weeds—interwoven growth. It was a favourite nesting place for the few shy birds that were native to British Columbia.

On the far side of the cemetery the Chinese had erected a great stone altar on which they placed whole pigs roasted and great piles of white cakes, looking like pure grease, to please the appetites of their dead who lay in rows in front of unpainted headboards with only Chinese characters written on them. The graves were as much alike as the Chinese themselves had been in clothes, pigtails and customs in life. There those foreigners lay, temporarily pitted, like winter vegetables. When there were bones enough they would all be gathered together from the graves and shipped back to China.

When the old Quadra Cemetery was quite full, its gates were closed and it was left to go entirely wild. Only the very tallest monuments could peer above the bushes. They seemed to say, "Hush!" as we children clattered past on our way to school.

Victoria had made a big new cemetery at Ross Bay, much farther out of town. Funerals took far longer then. The horses were not allowed to go faster than a walk as long as the corpse was behind them. They might trot as briskly as they liked back to town with the empty hearse behind them. Hayward's hearse had six enormous black plumes waving over the top of it. They swayed and writhed and were considered most dignified and in very good taste. Mr. Storey, the rival undertaker, had a hearse with six fuzzy black things on top having waists like the forms dress-makers use for fitting; they had woolly tails hanging down all round, waggling and lashing as the hearse went over the bumpy roads. They looked like six angry monkeys dancing over the coffin. Crêpe streamed from the hats of the under-taker, the driver, the widows' bonnets, the carriage whips and the knobs of the house doors where death waited for the hearse. The horses that dragged the dead were black and wore black plumes nodding on the top of their heads, black nets over their backs with drooping mournful fringes that ended in tassels tumbling over the shafts. Dead children had a little white hearse with white ponies and white nets and plumes. Funerals were made as slow and nodding and mournful as possible.

Every friend of the dead who owned a chaise or buggy and some hired hacks joined in the procession. Nobody thought of crossing the path of a funeral; people stood holding their hats in their hands with heads bowed patiently until the procession had passed. People drew down their front blinds as a funeral passed their houses. In Victoria the dead were buried as leisurely as the living lived.

The first graves in Ross Bay Cemetery looked very lonely and far apart, because Episcopalians could not lie beside Nonconformists, nor could Catholics rest beside Episcopalians. Methodists, Chinese, paupers buried by the City and people who believed in nothing at all, had to lie each in a separate part of the cemetery.

There were wide, gravelled driveways among the graves. Some of the graves were like little, low-walled gardens filled with flowers. This cemetery had a gravekeeper who kept the graves from getting muddled together with weeds and brambles.

But the waves of Ross Bay boomed against the cemetery bank and broke it. They bit into the earth, trying to wash out the coffins. They seemed to say, "I, the sea, can take better care of you, the dead, than the earth can. My gulls will cry over all of you alike. In me all denominations can mingle."

Schools

IT TOOK a generation and a half for English settlers in Victoria to accept the Canadian public school which they insisted on calling the "free school". They turned their noses up at our public schools as if they had been bad smells, preferring to send their children to old, ultra-genteel-hard-up English Ladies' Academies. Of these there were quite a few in Victoria; in them learning was confined to good manners. Politeness-education ladies had migrated to Canada, often in the hope of picking up bread and butter and possibly a husband, though they pretended all the while that they had come out on a very special mission—to teach the young of English-born gentlemen how not to become Canadian, to believe that all niceness and goodness came from ancestors and could have nothing to do with the wonderful new land, how not to acquire Colonial deportment, which was looked upon as crude, almost wicked. The only teaching qualifications these ladies possessed, and for their services they charged enormously, had been acquired by generations of habit.

So young ladies whose papas had sufficient means learned English manners—how to shut a door, how to bow gracefully, how to address people of their own class and how a servant, how to write a dignified letter in beautiful script, how to hold their heads up, their stomachs in and how to look down their noses at the right moment. For all this the old ladies were very handsomely remunerated and the girls' brains remained quite empty. Canadian public schools taught book learning but no manners to speak of.

My parents sent their two eldest daughters to a Ladies' Deportment Academy. Their next three children died before they were of school age. We four younger children were sent to the Public School. Father said we could "learn manners at home", but we could not get education in those days at the private school out west.

Later, Angela College, a Church School for girls, was built and endowed by Lady Burdett-Coutts. A red brick building, it stood on Church Hill. Education in it was costly. All our friends went to Angela College, but Father was by this time so prejudiced against private schools that he sent us to the Public School and was very much criticized for doing so. Our manners were watched closely and apprehensively by our friends. It hurt Mother but Father was proud that all his children, with the exception of me, were good students by Canadian standards. I hated school with the exception of the first two years when, being too young for so long a walk, I went to Mrs. Fraser's school for little girls near our own house.

Mrs. Fraser had large white teeth, a great many little dogs and a brother, Lennie, who kept house for her while she taught school. We sneaked potatoes out of Lennie's fry-pan as we trooped through the lean-to kitchen so as not to track dirt into Mrs. Fraser's front hall. The dunce stool was very comfortable—much more so than the wooden forms where the good pupils sat; I had ample opportunity of knowing. You could almost say the dunce's stool was specially mine.

The thing that I loved best at Mrs. Fraser's school was a big book of *Grimm's Fairy Tales* owned by a girl called Lizzie. At lunch time out in the mint bed in the backyard we went fairy and under the school desk when Mrs. Fraser was busy with a sick dog or a pupil's mama we seized other snatches.

By and by other English settlers began to send their children to the Public School and the High School too; then that old ladies' type of private school faded out of existence because education required a certain standard set by our

Public School system if people expected to obtain positions in Canada.

Those families who were able to send their sons and daughters to England to be "finished" did so. They came back more exaggeratedly English than the English themselves, "patering" and "matering" their father and mother, saying "Awfully jolly, don't you know!" and "No, not rawlly!" At first it seemed to us Canadians as if that "No" meant "You lie!" By and by, however, we found that it was only an English elegance in vogue just then.

Christmas

VICTORIA Christmas weather was always nippy—generally there was snow. We sewed presents for weeks before Christmas came—kettle holders, needle books, penwipers and cross-stitch bookmarkers. Just before Christmas we went out into the woods, cut down a fir tree and brought it home so alive still that the warm house fooled it into thinking spring had come, and it breathed delicious live pine smell all over the house. We put fir and holly behind all the pictures and on the mantelpiece and everywhere.

Plum puddings were dangling from under the pantry shelf by the tails of their boiling cloths. A month ago we had all sat round the breakfast-room table, stoning raisins while someone read a story aloud. Everyone had given the pudding a good-luck stir before it went into the bowls and was tied down and boiled for hours in the copper wash boiler while spicy smells ran all over the house. On Christmas Day the biggest pudding came out for a final boil before being brought to the table with brandy fire leaping up its sides from the dish, and with a sprig of holly scorching and crackling on its top.

Christmas Eve Father took us into town to see the shops lit up. Every lamp post had a fir tree tied to it—not corpsy old trees but fresh cut firs. Victoria streets were dark; this made the shops look all the brighter. Windows were decorated with mock snow made of cotton wool and diamond dust. Drygoods shops did not have much that was Christmassy to display except red flannel and rabbit fur baby coats and muffs and tippets. Chemists had immense globes

119

of red, green and blue medicine hanging from brass chains in their shop windows. I wished some of us could be sick enough for Dr. Helmcken to prescribe one of the splendid globes for us. The chemists also showed coloured soap and fancy perfume in bottles. Castor oil in hideous blue bottles peered from behind nice Christmas things and threw out hints about over-eating and stomach-ache. A horrid woman once told my mother that she let her children eat everything they wanted on Christmas Day and finished them up with a big dose of castor oil. Mr. Hibben, the stationer, was nicer than that woman and the chemist. He hid all the school books behind story books left open at the best pictures. He had "Merry Christmas" in cotton wool on red cardboard in his window.

It was the food shops that Merry Christmassed the hardest. In Mr. Saunders', the grocer's, window was a real Santa Claus grinding coffee. The wheel was bigger than he was. He had a long beard and moved his hands and his head. As the wheel went round the coffee beans went in, got ground, and came out, smell and all. In the window all round Santa were bonbons, cluster raisins, nuts and candied fruit, besides long walking-sticks made of peppermint candy. Next to this splendid window came Goodacre's horrible butcher shop—everything in it dead and naked. Dead geese and turkeys waggled, head down; dead beeves, calves and pigs straddled between immense meat hooks on the walls; naked sheep had bunches of coloured paper where their heads ought to have been and flowers and squiggles carved in the fat of their backs. Creatures that still had their heads on stared out of eyes like poached eggs when the white has run over the yolk. Baby pigs looked worst of all—pink and naked as bathing babies, their cheeks drawn back to make them smile at the red apples which had been forced into their toothless, sucking mouths. The shop floor was strewn deep in sawdust to catch blood drips. You heard no footsteps in the shop, only the sharpening of knives, sawing of bones, and bump, bump of the scale. Everybody was examining meat and saying, "Compliments of the Season" to everyone else, Father saying, "Fine display, Goodacre, very fine indeed!" We children rushed out and went back to Santa while Father chose his meat.

The shop of old George, the poulterer, was nearly as bad as Goodacre's, only the dead things did not look so dead, nor stare so hard, having shut the grey lids over their eyes to die. They were limp in necks and stiff in legs. As most of them had feathers on they looked like birds still, whereas the butcher's creatures had been rushed at once from life to meat.

The food shops ended the town, and after that came Johnson Street and Chinatown, which was full of black night. Here we turned back towards James' Bay, ready for bed.

There was a high mantelpiece in the breakfast room. And while we were hanging our stockings from it my sister read:

"'Twas the night before Christmas and all through the house

Not a creature was stirring, not even a mouse."

On the way to bed we could smell our Christmas tree waiting in the dining-room. The room was all dark but we knew that it stood on the floor and touched the ceiling and that it hung heavy with presents, ready for tomorrow. When the lights were lit there would be more of them than any of us children could count. We would all take hands and sing carols round the tree; Bong would come in and look with his mouth open. There was always things on it for him but he would not wait to get his presents. He would run back to his kitchen and we would take them to him there. It seemed as if Bong felt too Chinese to Christmas with us in our Canadian way.

The Presbyterian Church did not have service on Christmas morning so we went to the Reformed Episcopal with my sister; Father stayed home with Mother.

All the week before Christmas we had been in and out of a sort of hole under the Reformed Church, sewing twigs of pine onto long strips of brown paper. These were to be put round the church windows, which were very high. It was cold under the church and badly lighted. We all sneezed and hunted round for old boards to put beneath our feet on the earth floor under the table where we sat pricking ourselves with holly, and getting stuck up with pine gum. The pricking made the ladies' words sharp—that and their sniffy colds and remembering all the work to be done at home. Everything unusual was fun for us children. We felt important helping to decorate the Church.

Present-giving was only done to members in one's immediate family. Others you gave love and a card to, and kissed the people you did not usually kiss.

New Year's Day had excitement too. It was the custom for ladies to stay at home, sitting in their drawing-rooms with decanters of wine and fine cakes handy. Gentlemen called to wish them the "Compliments of the Season". Right after lunch we went up to Mother's room where you could see farthest down the street, to watch for Mother's first caller, and it was always the shy Cameron brothers, coming very early so as to avoid other visitors.

Gentlemen paid their respects at Government House, too, on New Year's Day, and Naval officers made a point of returning the hospitality of those who had entertained them while stationed in Victoria.

Regatta

THE BEAUTIFUL Gorge waters were smooth as glass once Victoria Harbour had been crossed. The Gorge was an arm of the sea which ran into the land for three miles. Near its head was a narrow rocky pass with a hidden rock in the centre which capsized many a canoe and marooned many a picnic party above the Gorge until long after midnight, for when the tide was running in or out through the pass there was a four-foot fall with foam and great roaring. A bridge ran across from one side of the Gorge to the other, high above the water. The banks on both sides of the Arm were heavily wooded; a few fine homes snuggled among the trees and had gardens running to the water. Most of the other property was public—anyone could picnic on it.

The waters of the Gorge were much warmer than the water of the beaches round Victoria. Jones' Boathouse beside James' Bay Bridge rented out boats and canoes; many people living along the harbour front had boathouses and boats of their own, for regattas and water sports were one of Victoria's chief attractions. Visitors came from Vancouver and from the States on the 24th of May to see them.

The Navy and the Indian tribes up and down the Coast took part in the races, the Navy rowing their heavy ship's boats round from Esquimalt Harbour, manned by blue-jackets, while smart little pinnaces "pip-pipped" along commanded by young midshipmen. The Indians came from long distances in their slender, racing dugout canoes—ten paddles and a steersman to each canoe.

The harbour was gay with flags. Races started from the Gorge Bridge at 1 p.m. Our family went to the Regatta with Mr. and Mrs. Bales. Mr. Bales had a shipyard just below Point Ellice Bridge, at the beginning of the Arm waters. We got into Mr. Bales' boat at the shipyard where unfinished boats stood all round us just above high tide. They looked as we felt when we shivered in our nightgowns on Beacon Hill beaches waiting for the courage to dip into the sea. But rosy-faced Mr. Bales eased his boats gently into the water; he did not seize and duck them as my big sister did us.

When the picnic was all stowed into Mr. Bales' boat we pushed out into the stream and joined the others—sail boats, canoes, rafts and fish boats, all nosing their way up the Gorge along with the naval boats and war canoes. There were bands and mouth-organs, concertinas and flags. The Indian families in their canoes glided very quietly except for an occasional yapping from one of their dogs when he saw a foe in another canoe.

There was the hollow rumble of traffic over Point Ellice Bridge as we passed under it. Dust sprinkled down between the planks and fell on us. Out-of-town people came to the Regatta in wagons and buggies, driving up the Gore Road on one side of the Arm or the Craigflower Road on the other side, tying their horses in the bush and carrying their picnic baskets through the woods to the shore. People lit small fires and picnicked near the water's edge where they could see the races pass.

The races started from the Gorge Bridge, came down the Arm, turned round Deadman's Island, an old Indian burial ground, and returned to the bridge.

The Indian canoe races were the most exciting of all the Regatta. Ten paddles dipped as one paddle, ten men bent as one man, while the steersman kept time for them with grunting bows. The men had bright coloured shirts and gay head-bands; some even had painted faces. The

Kloochman's was an even grander race than the Indian men's. Solid, earnest women with gay shawls wound round their middles gave every scrap of themselves to the canoe; it came alive and darted through the water like a flash, foam following the paddles. The dips, heaves and grunts of all the women were only one dip, heave and grunt. Watchers from the banks yelled; the Indians watched from their canoes by the shore, with an intent, silent stare.

The Bluejacket Races were fine, too. Each boat was like a stout, brave monster, enduring and reliable—the powerful, measured strokes of the British Navy, sure and unerring as the earth itself, not like the cranky war canoes, flashing through their races like running fire.

At the end of the Regatta came something mean and cruel. An old hulk was towed to midstream; a long pole hung over the water at one end of her, and, suspended from its tip, was a crate crammed full of agonized pig squeals. The pole was greased and men tried to walk out to the end of it and dislodge the crate. The pole was supple, the crate swayed as each man crept out clinging desperately and finally fell off into the sea. The terrified pig in the crate squealed. People roared with laughter and greasers applied fresh grease for the next person's try. When at last a man was successful and with a great splash crate and pig plunged into the sea, sailors hurried to pull it into a boat before poor pig drowned.

The band blared, "God Save The Queen" and everyone on the banks and in the boats raised their hats and sang with the band. "Queen! Queen!" echoed back from the trees and the rocks.

The wet, shivering pig in his crate did not care whether the Queen were saved or not. "God save *me!*" was his imploring squeal.

Characters

STRANGE characters came to little Victoria. It seemed as if people who could not fit in anywhere else arrived here sooner or later till Victoria poked, bulged and hollowed over queer shapes of strange people, as a snake, swallowing its food whole, looks lumpy during digestion. Victoria had some hard lumps to digest.

Sometimes they came, hurried by a firm push from behind given by relatives in the Old Country, around whose necks they had hung too heavily for many years, and who said, "Now that travel is so easy, why not, dear? . . . Door to door without a stop! . . . Such an adventure! Victoria is a crown colony, not Canadian—try it, darling!" So the "darlings" whose lives from birth had been humdrum, especially since the rest of the family had married and left the old home to them and nothing for its upkeep, nibbled at the thought, grabbed for the word "adventure", sold up and sailed. Relatives saw them off, calling them "old sports", begging them to write—they, who had never had anything to write about in their whole lives were now launched proudly into adventure.

Sometimes it was a bachelor brother and spinster sister of the glued-together type of family remnants.

After the whistle shrieked every mile of water washed the old land away fainter and fainter and hurried them into the unknown. They began to ache—such vast quantities of water! Such vast quantities of land! The ache grew and grew. By and by they saw the western forests and the little town of Victoria drowned in silent loneliness; there was then no describing how they felt. They rented uncomfortable, mean little cottages or shacks and did with incompetent hands what well-trained Old Country servants had all their lives done for them. Too late! Turning back was impossible; the old home was sold, its price already seeping away too fast. There were many of these sad people in Victoria, shuddering when they saw a Western funeral, thinking of the cosiness of Old Country churchyards.

There were maiden aunts, who had attached themselves to the family circle of a married brother and who undertook the diction and deportment of his children, bitterly regretting the decision of Brother to migrate to Canada, but never for one moment faltering in their duty to Brother's family, standing between his children and colonialism. The Maiden Aunts swallowed their crosses with a difficult gulp. Auntie's job was discounted in the New World; Canadian-born children soon rebelled at her tyranny. She sank into a wilted homesick derelict, sniffling by the fireside while the mother learned more or less to work with her own hands, so that she could instruct what Auntie called her "heathen help" in kitchen low art. Auntie herself refused to acknowledge base presences such as cook-stoves and wash-tubs.

In our family there were no maiden aunts. Our delicate little Mother had six living children and three dead ones and, with the help of her older daughters and the Chinese boy, Bong, we managed very comfortably without aunts. Many a useless servant-dependent woman from the Old Country was shown by my mother how to use her own hands and her own brain in her Canadian home with no other help than green Chinese boys.

In Toronto Street over James' Bay way there lived a most astonishing family, consisting of two brothers, Fat O'Flahty and Lean O'Flahty and a sister, Miss O'Flahty. All were above middle age. They built a shanty entirely of driftwood which they gathered and hauled from the beach. They might be seen any hour of the day or night trundling logs home on a wheel-barrow, taking long rests on its handle while they smoked a pipe. The brothers never sawed the driftwood but used it any length, just as it came out of the sea—mostly longish, round tree trunks rubbed smooth by rocks and sea on their long swims, where from no one knew.

The O'Flahty's house looked like a bonfire heaped ready for lighting. The only place where the wood of the entire shanty was halfway level was at the ground and even there it was bumpy. The up ends of all the logs higgledy-piggledied into the sky, some logs long, some short. The door was made of derelict planks gathered on the beach, too, and the roof was of anything at all—mostly of tin cans. It had a stovepipe sticking through the top. The fence round the O'Flahty's small piece of ground was built to match the house.

The O'Flahtys had lived in this strange house for some years when Mother heard that Miss O'Flahty was very ill. She sent us post haste down, with some soup. We knocked on the gate which was padlocked. Fat O'Flahty came and let us in. We walked on a plank up to the door which was also padlocked.

"She's bad," he said and led the way into the shanty.

It was nearly dark and very smoky. In the centre of the one room stood a jumble of drift logs standing upright to make a little room. Fat O'Flahty moved two logs aside and, when we were accustomed to the dark, we saw a white patch lying in the corner. It was Miss O'Flahty's face. Her bed was made of logs too. It was built on the floor and had no legs. There was no space for us to step inside Miss O'Flahty's bedroom. There was scarcely room for even our looks to squeeze in.

Fat O'Flahty behind my sister said, "Does she look awful sick?" and Lean O'Flahty peering behind Fat with some of the soup in a tin cup, said also, "Does she seem turrible bad?" Their voices were frightened. Lean O'Flahty held the tin cup of soup towards the sick woman. The dim patch of white face in the corner shook a feeble "No". The brothers groaned.

Miss O'Flahty died. Lean and Fat had her embalmed and put her into a handsome casket. She rode to the Outer Wharf in the same wheel-barrow which had lugged their building wood from the beach. The brothers trundled it. We were down at the Outer Wharf, seeing Auntie away by the San Francisco boat. "Ouch! It's a coffin!" squealed Auntie as her cloak brushed it. Fat and Lean O'Flahty were sitting one on either handle of the barrow, crying. When all were aboard, the brothers, each with a fist in his eye and with loud sniffs, wheeled the coffin down between decks and the O'Flahty family disappeared. Next time we passed down Toronto Street their crazy house was gone too.

Another human derelict was Elizabeth Pickering—she wore a bright red shawl and roamed the streets of Victoria, intoxicated most of the time. Occasionally she sobered briefly and went to the kindly Bishop to ask help. The Bishop handed her over to his maiden sister who specialized in correction. Elizabeth would settle herself comfortably, drawing a chair to the fire to toast her toes and doze till she became thirsty again. Then, with a great yawn, she would reach for the little packages the Bishop's wife had put near her on the table. Regardless of whether Aunt Cridge had finished her lecture on drink or not she would rise with a sympathetic, "Feelin' yer rheumatics today, baint ye, pore soul? Me and you suffers the same—its crool!"

Old Teenie was another familiar figure of our school days. Teenie was half negro—half crazy. Her hut was on Fort Street in the centre of a rough field and lay a little below street level. Boys used to throw stones onto her tin roof and then run away. Out came old Teenie, buzzing mad as a whole nest of wasps. Muttered awfulnesses came from her great padded bonnet. It shook, her tatters shook, so did wisps of grey hair and old Teenie's pair of tiny black fists.

I don't know who looked after Teenie. She scoured with

stick and sack the ditches and empty lots, putting oddments into her sack, shaking her stick at everyone, muttering, always muttering.

Nobody questioned where these derelicts came from. They were taken as much for granted as the skunk cabbages in our swamps.

Victoria's queer people were not all poor, either—there were doddering old gentlemen. I can remember them driving about Victoria in their little buggies—the fatter the man, the smaller the buggy! They had old nursemaid horses who trundled them as faithfully as any mammy does her baby in its pram. Every day, wet or fine, the horses aired their old men on Dallas Road. Knowing that their charges slept through the entire outing, the faithful creatures never moved from the middle of the road nor changed from a slow walk. The public also knew by the lolling heads and slack reins that the old men slept and gave their buggies right of way. Street traffic was not heavy, time no object. Chaises, gentlemen's high dog-carts passed the nursemaid horses briskly. The dog-carts paused at roadhouse bars and again overtook the patient plodding horses who walked their charges to a certain tree on Foul Bay Road, circled it and strolled home again just as the old men's Chinese cooks put their dinner on the table. The old horses were punctual to the dot.

One of these old men was very fond of children. When he met us, if he happened to be awake, he pulled up with a wheezy "Whoa", meant both for us and for his horse. Taking a screw of paper from his pocket he bent over the wheel and gave us each a lollipop and a smile. He was so ugly that we were afraid, but Mother, who knew who he was told us he loved children and that it was all right. If, however, we saw his buggy coming in time we hid until it was past; he was such a very ugly old man!

A family we knew had one of those "Papa's-sister" Aunts who took it upon herself to be a corrector of manners not only for her own nieces but for young Canadians in general. In fact she aspired to introduce elegance into the Far West. This elegant and energetic lady walked across Beacon Hill at seven-thirty on fine summer mornings, arriving at our house in time for family prayers and breakfast. In spite of her erect carriage she could flop to her knees to pray as smart as any of us. That over, she kissed us all round, holding each at arm's length and with popping, piercing eyes, criticized our tooth-brushing, our hair ribbons, our finger nails, recommended that we eat more porridge or less, told Mother to give us no raw fruit at all, always to stew it, no stone fruit at all, no candy, told us never to ask for second helps, but wait to be invited, had us do a little English pronouncing, then, having made us late, said, "Hurry! hurry! Lateness is unpardonable, dears! Ladies are never late."

Then there were Brother Charlie and Sister Tilly, evidently sworn each to see other into the grave. This pair minced up Birdcage Walk like elderly fowls, holding their heads each a little to one side—Charlie so that Tilly's lips could reach his deaf ear, Tilly so that she might direct her shriek straight into Charlie's drum. The harder she shrieked the higher she squeaked. Charlie, on the other hand, was far too gentlemanly to speak in public places above a whisper which he could not hear himself, so he felt it safest always to say "Yes, yes, dear Tilly" or "Exactly so, Tilly dear" when he should often have said, "No, Tilly, certainly not!"

Brother and sister whispered and squeaked up Birdcage Walk where they lived. They hopped up the two steps to the inset door of their cottage and cooed themselves in.

"Yes, yes, dear Tilly, yes!"

Loyalty

MEDINA'S GROVE was a gentle place; its moist mildness
softened even the starch in Father and begged the twinkle
that sat behind his stern grey eyes to come out. The Grove
had not the sombre weight that belongs to the forest, nor
had it the bare coldness of a windswept clearing. It was
beautifully half real, like the place you fall into after the
candle is blown out, and sleep is just taking hold of you.

Victoria had to be specially loyal because she was named
after the Queen. To her the most important day, after Christmas Day of course, was the Queen's Birthday, on the
twenty-fourth of May. We made more fuss over the Queen's
Birthday than did any other town in Canada.

May is just about our most lovely month. The lilacs,
the hawthorn, the laburnums and the broom are all in
blossom, just begging the keen Spring winds to let their
petals hang on till after the twenty-fourth so that Victoria
can look most splendid for the Queen's Birthday. On the
twenty-third, one often had to stand on the chopping block
and, hanging onto the verandah post with rain spittering
in your face, sing right up into the sky—

> "Rain, rain go away.
> Come again another day
> When I cook and when I bake
> I'll send you up a patty-cake."

Sometimes the rain listened, sometimes it did not. But most
of our twenty-fourths were fine which was lucky because

132

on the Queen's Birthday we wore our Summer frocks for the first time.

Mother prepared a splendid picnic. Father left his business frown and his home sternness behind him. Rugs, food and the black billy for making tea, were packed into the old baby buggy and we trundled it straight down Simcoe Street. Simcoe Street passed the side of our place and ended in Medina's Grove. In May, what with the new green on the bushes, the Medina's calves skipping about, and Medina Grove birds nesting, it was like fairy land. Sea air blew in from the beach, just one field away! Seagulls swooped down to look for picnic bits. The ground was all bumpy from being crowded with more new grass than the cows could eat. There were some big trees in the Grove, but not thick enough to keep the sun out. Every kind of delicious spring smell was there. It was not like being in a garden to play; the Grove was gently wild but had not the awe of the forest. Bushes grew here in little groups like families. Each picnic could have its own place quite private; just the laughs tumbled through the bushes and mixed. There were no gates to remember to shut, no flower beds you must not scoot across. You might pick anything you liked and eat as much picnic as you could. These Medina Grove picnics were our first Queen's Birthdays. By and by we grew older and steady enough to sit still in boats; then we went to regattas, up the Arm, on the twenty-fourth. The Queen's Birthday changed then. It was not so much our own day. A shadowy little old lady owned it.

This Queen, after whom Victoria was named, did not mean any more to me than a name. The older ones knew all about her and so I suppose they thought I did. It was Mrs. Mitchell who made the Royal Family stop being fairy and turned Royalty into real live people for me. Mrs. Mitchell was a little, frail, old woman. Henry, her husband, was an English nurseryman. They came from England and started a nursery garden not far from our house, at the time when farm land was being cut into small personal pieces. Mother went to see any new people who came to live near us, if she saw that they were lonely and homesick. Mrs. Mitchell was very homesick and very lonely. She said she loved me from the first time my Mother took me to see her, because I was fat and rosy just like an English child. But I was not an English child and I didn't love her because she was English. I loved Mrs. Mitchell because she loved creatures, and I loved her garden, too, with its long rows of nursery stock, and its beds of pinks and mignonette. Mrs. Mitchell was gentle, small and frail. She had a little weak voice, which squeaked higher and higher the more she loved. Her guinea fowl and I cracked it altogether. She had four speckled guinea fowl—she and Henry loved them as if they had been real children. They opened the door of their cottage and called, "Coom, coom, coom, pretty little dears"—and the guineas came mincing through the kitchen into the sitting-room, and jumped into their laps.

The Mitchells' nursery garden was next to a farm rented by Jim Phillips. Jim got angry because the guinea fowl flew over the fence into his grain field and he shot three of them. The old couple cried and cried. They took it to law and got the price of the guineas but the price of the birds' flesh meant nothing to them. It was the life gone from their birds that they cried for. Never having any children the guineas had been next best. This last bird of their four they never let out of their sight. Jim Phillips was furious that he had to pay for the bodies of the other three especially as he knew it was only for love, not value, that they cried.

Mrs. Mitchell cuddled the last bird in her little black silk apron and bowing her head on his speckled back cried into his feathers mournfully rocking him and herself. She took the little pink bow out of her black lace cap and its long black ties dropped over her shoulders as she bent crying. There was always a little bunch of everlasting flowers sewn into her cap over one ear, brittle, dried up little things like chrisalises; she let these be. She had a whole floor of everlasting flowers spread to dry in her front room. They smelled like hay and were just as much alive after they had been dead for a whole year. She made wreaths of them for funerals. Everlasting flowers reminded people there was no death, she said.

I went very often to Mrs. Mitchell to try to cheer her over the guinea fowl, but it seemed I could not cheer her at all. The remaining guinea's wings were all drooped with loneliness and she held him in her lap nearly all day. I looked around the sitting-room to find something happy to say. The walls were covered with pictures of gentlemen and ladies cut out of the *London News* and the *Daily Graphic*. Grand ladies with frizzled hair and lots of necklaces, men with medals on and sashes across their chests.

"Q-u-e-e-n V-i-c-t-o-r-i-a", I spelled out.

"Is that the lady who has the twenty-fourth of May birthday?"

"Yes my dear," Mrs. Mitchell sniffled into the guinea's feathers. "Yes, our most gracious Queen Victoria."

"Who is the man beside her?"

"The late Prince Consort, my dear, and this is the Princess Royal, and here is the Prince of Wales and Princess Beatrice."

"Who *are* these people?" I asked. "I thought Princes and Princesses just belonged to fairy tales. What have they to do with Queen Victoria?"

Mrs. Mitchell was very much shocked indeed. She stopped crying and, using the guinea fowl as a pointer, she went from picture to picture telling the bird and me who all the Royalties were, how old, whom they had married and so on. At last we came to a lady in a black frame with a bow of crêpe over the top of it and a bunch of everlasting flowers underneath. "Princess Alice", said Mrs. Mitchell with a long, long sniffle, "now a blessed saint," and she began to cry all over again.

I thought these picture people must be relatives of Mrs. Mitchell's, she seemed to know them so well and cried so hard about Alice. The Queen's picture was everywhere. I knew she was someone tremendous, though to me she had been vague and far off like Job or St. Paul. I had never known she was real and had a family, only that she owned

Victoria, Canada, and the twenty-fourth of May, the Church of England and all the soldiers and sailors in the world. Now suddenly she became real—a woman like Mother with a large family.

Mrs. Mitchell took a great deal of pains to get the Royal family straight in my head and it was lucky she did, because who should come out to Canada, to Victoria, that very year and pay a long visit to Government House, but the Princess Louise and the Marquis of Lorne! This excited Mrs. Mitchell so that she stopped crying. She, who never went out, found a bonnet that I had never seen before, put a dolman over her best silk dress, locked the guinea fowl safe in her kitchen and got into a hack with Henry, her smelling-bottle and her cap, in which was a new bunch of everlasting flowers. The cap was in a paper bag on Henry's knee. They drove to the house of Dr. Ashe on Fort Street where the procession was to pass and sat in a bow window and waved at the Princess. When she saw the Princess smiling and dressed in gay colours, she realized that her beloved Princess Alice had been dead longer than she thought and that Court mourning was finished. She went home and took the crêpe off Alice but she left the everlasting flowers.

Mrs. Mitchell watched the papers for every crumb of news of her Princess while the visitors were in Victoria—how she had gone sketching in the Park, how she used to go into the shops and chat with people; how once she went into a bake-shop to buy some cakes and stepped behind the counter to point out the kind to the baker who ordered her back, saying gruffly, "Nobody ain't allowed behind my counter, mum," and then when she gave the address, the baker nearly died of shame and so did Mrs. Mitchell as she read it.

Seeing Royalty waked again all Mrs. Mitchell's homesickness for England. They sold everything and she and Henry went back to the Old Country to die. She gave me a doctor's book on diseases and an empty box with a lock and key. I did not like the disease book and could never find anything important enough to lock up in the box; so I put it away on a high shelf. Mrs. Mitchell cried dreadfully when she left Victoria but kept saying "I'm going home, my dear, going home."

The journey nearly killed her, and England did quite. All her people were dead except distant cousins. England was different from what she had remembered. She sent me Gray's *Elegy in a Country Churchyard* and Henry wrote saying she was crying for me and for Victoria now as she had cried for England and Princess Alice and the guinea fowl. Then came a silver and black card "In Memoriam to Anne Mitchell"—then I had something to lock away in the little box, with a little bunch of everlasting flowers, the last that Mrs. Mitchell gave me.

Doctor and Dentist

WHEN VICTORIA was young specialists had not been invented —the Family Doctor did you all over. You did not have a special doctor for each part. Dr. Helmcken attended to all our ailments—Father's gout, our stomach-aches; he even told us what to do once when the cat had fits. If he was wanted in a hurry he got there in no time and did not wait for you to become sicker so that he could make a bigger cure. You began to get better the moment you heard Dr. Helmcken coming up the stairs. He did have the most horrible medicines—castor oil, Gregory's powder, blue pills, black draughts, sulphur and treacle.

Jokey people called him Dr. Heal-my-skin. He had been Doctor in the old Fort and knew everybody in Victoria. He was very thin, very active, very cheery. He had an old brown mare called Julia. When the Doctor came to see Mother we fed Julia at the gate with clover. The Doctor loved old Julia. One stormy night he was sent for because Mother was very ill. He came very quickly and Mother said, "I am sorry to bring you and Julia out on such a night, Doctor."

"Julia is in her stable. What was the good of two of us getting wet?" he replied.

My little brother fell across a picket fence once and tore his leg. The Doctor put him on our dining-room sofa and sewed it up. The Chinaboy came rushing in to say, "House all burn up!" Dr. Helmcken put in the last stitch, wiped his needle on his coat sleeve and put it into his case, then, stripping off his coat, rushed to the kitchen pump and pumped till the fire was put out.

Once I knelt on a needle which broke into my knee. While I was telling Mother about it who should come up the steps but the Doctor! He had just looked in to see the baby who had not been very well. They put me on the kitchen table. The Doctor cut slits in my knee and wiggled his fingers round inside it for three hours hunting for the pieces of needle. They did not know the way of drawing bits out with a magnet then, nor did they give chloroform for little things like that.

The Doctor said, "Yell, lassie, yell! It will let the pain out." I did yell, but the pain stayed in.

I remember the Doctor's glad voice as he said, "Thank God, I have got all of it now, or the lassie would have been lame for life with that under her knee cap!" Then he washed his hands under the kitchen tap and gave me a peppermint.

Dr. Helmcken knew each part of every one of us. He could have taken us to pieces and put us together again without mixing up any of our legs or noses or anything.

Dr. Helmcken's office was a tiny two-room cottage on the lower end of Fort Street near Wharf Street. It sat in a hummocky field; you walked along two planks and came to three steps and the door. The outer room had a big table in the centre filled with bottles of all sizes and shapes. All were empty and all dusty. Round the walls of the room were shelves with more bottles, all full, and lots of musty old books. The inner office had a stove and was very higgledy-piggledy. He would allow no one to go in and tidy it up.

The Doctor sat in a round-backed wooden chair before a table; there were three kitchen chairs against the wall for invalids. He took you over to a very dirty, uncurtained window, jerked up the blind and said, "Tongue!" Then he poked you round the middle so hard that things fell out of your pockets. He put a wooden trumpet bang down on your chest and stuck his ear to the other end. After listening and grunting he went into the bottle room, took a bottle, blew the dust off it and emptied out the dead flies. Then he went to the shelves and filled it from several other bottles, corked it, gave it to Mother and sent you home to get well on it. He stood on the step and lit a new cigar after every patient as if he was burning up your symptoms to make room for the next sick person.

Victoria's dentist was a different sort of person. He shammed. "Toothache, eh?" he said in a "pretend" sorry voice with his nose twisted against one cheek or the other as if he felt the pain most awfully himself. He sat you in a green plush chair and wound you up to his eye. Then he took your head in his wide red hand that smelled of fancy soap and pushed back your cheek, saying, "Let me just see —I am not going to do anything." All the time he was taking something from a tray behind you and, before you knew where you were, he had nearly pulled the head off your neck.

I shouted, "You lied!" and got slapped as well as extracted, while the blood ran down my chin.

My Father never had a toothache till he was sixty years of age, nor did he lose a tooth. When the dentist said four of my second teeth needed to be filled, Father said, "Nonsense! Pull them out." The dentist said it was a shame to pull the teeth and his shamming nose twisted; but all the time he was looking over my head at my pretty sister who had taken me. He grabbed my head; I clenched my teeth. They bribed me with ten cent pieces and apples till I opened and then I was sorry and bit down on his fingers.

I knew a girl who liked the dentist, but she had only had her teeth filled, never pulled, and he gave her candy. One day she said to me, "I wonder what the dentist's name is? His initials are R.B."

"I know. It is Royal Beast," I said.

Beast was a word we were never allowed to use. I always called the dentist "Royal Beast" after that. It made me feel much better.

Chain Gang

THE TWO sisters a lot older than I taught the two sisters a little older about many things, but when I was old enough to puzzle over these same things and to ask questions I was told, "Don't pester! Don't ask questions just for the sake of asking." But two years and four years make a lot of difference in the sense and understanding of a small girl. At six I was not able to grasp what eight and ten could, so there were gaps in my knowing and a great many things that I only half understood such as Saloons, and the Royal Family, and the Chain Gang.

One day we were going to town with my big sister and passed a lot of men working at the roadside by the Parliament Buildings. They wore unusual clothes and had little round caps on top of heads shaved so close they looked like peeled apples stuck on top of their bodies. They sat on big rocks and crushed smaller rocks into little bits with sharp pointed hammers—Crack, tap! Crack, tap! Two men stood behind the workers watching their every move. Each held a gun and never took his eyes off them for one moment, staring as hard as the men stared at the stones. Nobody's stare shifted and nobody spoke. There was only the unhappy tap, tap of the little hammers and the slow roll of each piece of rock rolling down the little stone piles, falling at the feet of the men like enormous stone tears.

I looked up at my sister to ask but she gave me a "hush-frown" and dragged me quickly past. We had just got on to James' Bay Bridge when there was a clank, clank and a tramp, tramp, tramp behind us. The queer men were being marched into town and the two men with the guns were marching one in front and one behind them, watching as hard as ever. One leg of each man had a dragging limp. Then I saw that every man had a bar of iron fastened to one leg at the knee and again at the ankle. It took a long time for them to catch up to us and pass. We walked on the other side of the foot rail of the bridge. My sister was very put out at having to march beside the men: you could not help keeping time to the jangling tramp. We crossed Bastion Street on the way to Father's store and came to an immense, close board fence with spikes on the top, which I had never noticed before. The fence broke suddenly into a gate which swallowed the marching men, shutting with a snap that cut off the limping clank before I could get even a peep of what was inside it. There was a red brick building with barred windows beside the fence. Again I looked up at my sister. "Jail," she said—"Chain Gang."

When Victoria was so nearly a city that there were many roads to be built, the town bought a noisy monster called "Lizzie". Lizzie snorted up to a rock pile and they fed her chunks of rock in iron buckets which ran round on a chain. She chewed and spat, chewed and spat until the rocks were ready for road making. So now the Chain Gang did not have to sit by the roadside and smack rocks any longer. Lizzie chewed instead and the Gang now worked on the grounds of Government House and the Parliament Buildings.

"Lizzie" fed for a very long time on Marvin's Hill on the James' Bay side of the mud flats. It had an immense quantity of rock. Horses hated the steepness of Marvin's Hill: the heavy chaises slipped back. The smart old horses zig-zagged them up sideways, pretending that they were not trying to climb a hill at all but just having fun making snake fence patterns in the deep dust.

Marvin's Hill and Church Hill frowned hard at each other; the mud flats, all soft and smelly, smiled between them. Blanshard Street dipped down Marvin's Hill and up

Church Hill again. The deepest part of its dip was from Humboldt Street on the north to the top of Marvin's Hill. The town built a high sidewalk on stilts which made the climb for walking people easier. We went over the high sidewalk every Sunday on the way to church. It was the most exciting part of the two-mile walk. From the high sidewalk you looked out across the flats to James' Bay Bridge. There was a row of cabins on Humboldt Street. It was called Kanaka Row: the cabins rested their chins on the street and their hind legs stuck high out of the mud behind. Working men with Indian wives lived in Kanaka Row and Sunday was the day for the women to wash the men's clothes. The men lazed in bed while their shirts and pants flapped on clothes lines high over the mud.

On the corner of Humboldt and Blanshard stood the Reformed Episcopal Church; criss-cross from it was the White Horse Saloon. A great brick drain ran under Blanshard Street, gushing into the slough which rambled over the mud flats and out to the sea. Above the flats on the Belville Street side were Governor Douglas's and Doctor Helmcken's houses. There was always plenty to be seen from the high sidewalk. The Reformed Episcopal Sunday School was beside the church. It was sure to be either going in or coming out as we passed. There were splendid slides on either side of its steps which must have spoiled heaps of boys' Sunday pants. Below the schoolhouse was a jungle of sweet-briar rose bushes and then came the mud, covered round the edges with coarse marsh grass.

There were nearly always Indians camped on the Flats. They drew their canoes up the slough. Some camped right in their canoes with a canvas tent across the top, some pitched tents on the higher ground. The smoke of their camp fires curled up. Indians loved camping here because for many, many years the mud flats were used as the town's rubbish dump. Square blue carts backed to the edge of Blanshard Street and spattered their loads overboard—old clothes, old stoves, broken baby buggies, broken crockery and beds. The Indians picked it all over, chose what they could use, stowed it away in their canoes to take to their houses. When the tide came up and flooded the slough and flats the canoes slipped away, the Indians calling to their dogs who lingered for a last pick among the rubbish. Then they waded through the mud and caught up with the canoes just before they reached the sea. You got excited watching to see if they'd make it.

The last and very meanest pick of all the rubbish was left to the screeching seagulls that swooped for the dregs of refuse, rising triumphant as kings with new crowns.

From the high sidewalk you could see all this besides looking down into the Convent garden lying on the other side of the raised walk. Here the Convent Sisters marched two and two along the garden paths with a long snake of boarders wiggling in front of them, in and out among flower beds. The nuns' veils billowed and flapped behind the snaky line of girls as if the sisters were shooing the serpent from the Garden of Eden.

At the top of Marvin's Hill, gaunt and quiet, stood the rock-chewing monster, "Lizzie". She did not chew on Sundays. Father measured how much she had done since last Sunday. He was stern about Lizzie. She was an American notion. She had cost the town a lot of money—Father was a tax-payer and a good citizen.

Cook Street

COOK STREET crossed Fort Street just before the point at which a better class of houses mounted the Fort Street Hill and made it residential.

A few semi-nice houses did trickle round the corner of Fort into Cook but they got smaller, poorer and scarcer as Cook Street went south. At Fairfield Road Cook stopped being a street at all except on the town map in the City Hall. In reality, from Fairfield Road to the sea, it was nothing but a streak of skunk-cabbage bog running between King's and Smith's dairy farms. Cows peered through the farm fence bars at the luscious greenery in the "street" where bushes were so snarled and tangled together that down there in the greasy bog among the skunk cabbages they could not tell which root was theirs.

In summertime the swamp dried out somewhat, enough at least for the stout shoes of school children to tramp a crooked little path through its centre. Skirting puddles and nobbledy roots, among which lurked dank smells of cat-flower and skunk cabbages, this path was a short cut to school.

In winter, if there was much rain, this so-called "Street" and the low-lying fields on either side lay all drowned together under a stretch of water which was called King's Pond. After several good frosts people went there to skate.

When James' Bay mud flats had become too "towny" to be a rubbish heap any more, the little two-wheeled, one-horse dump-carts trundled their loads of garbage to the unmade end of Cook Street and spilled it among the boggy ooze. Each load of rubbish built foothold as it went. The horse clung with his hooves to the last load while he spilt the next. The little blue carts tipped and splattered, tipped and splattered their contents over the edge. Every load helped to build a foundation for Cook Street, rubbish pounded to solidity by horses' hooves and children's boots. The street formed slowly, working from its middle and firming gradually to the fence on either side. Occasionally clay discarded from some building excavation was thrown on top to solidify wash boilers and stoves, old kettles and beds. It took all our school years for rusty iron to flake into dust. Soft things rotted and grew fungi or dissolved to a kind of jelly which by and by hardened and powdered to dust.

It took years to steady the underneath of Cook Street between Fairfield and Dallas Road. Here the map said that Cook Street stopped and the sea bounced and bellowed along the pebbly beach under the cliffs.

When I exercised the pony, old Johnny, after school hours I loved to ride through the Cook Street chaos of garbage. High and safe on the horse's back I could look down into it and see wild rose bushes forcing their blooms up through lidless cook stoves and skunk cabbage peeping out of bottomless perambulators, beds tipped at any angle, their years of restfulness all finished and done with.

The harder the town grew, the more back-door rubbish there was. The clay-coloured, padded bonnet of half-crazy, half-negro old Teenie bobbed among the garbage while her stick poked and her claw-like hands clutched, ramming gleanings into her sack with derelict mutterings scarcely more audible than the click of disintegration amongst the decay in which she rooted. Teenie herself belonged to this sisterhood of discards. Back in her cabin she poured what she had rescued from her sack onto the floor, muttering and gibbering to the castoffs as if they were her friends.

At last the emptiness was flattened out of every discard, the chinks between were filled up with clay and Cook Street was hard and level; the Town drained and paved it and it became a finished highway running from the town to the sea. New houses set their faces to it, houses with flower gardens in front. All its old cow farms moved out into the country.

Our town now had a mature garbage system which towed our horribles out to sea in barges. It seemed, though, that the old kettles and much of the rubbish got homesick; back they danced patiently riding wave after wave to the beach below Cook Street to lie there, hideous in broken nakedness, no soft spread of greenery to hide their ugliness.

As Cook Street progressed from cow farm to residential district she had a spell of being Chinese vegetable gardens. In the fields on either side patient, blue-jean figures worked from dawn till dark, bending over the soil, planting, weeding, watering by hand from wells. The water was carried in five-gallon coal oil cans, one on either end of a bamboo pole slung over the Chinaman's shoulder. He stood the load among his vegetable rows and dipped a little to each plant.

When his vegetables were ready to market, the Chinaman put them into great bamboo baskets slung on each end of his pole. As he had carried water to his plants, so he carried vegetables to townspeople, going from door to door joggety-trot with baskets swaying.

Waterworks

THOSE Victorians who did not have a well on their own place bought water by the bucket from the great barrel water-cart which peddled it. Water brought in wooden pipes from Spring Ridge on the northern outskirts of the town was our next modernness. Three wonderful springs watered Victoria, one on Spring Ridge, one in Fairfield and one at Beacon Hill. People carried this sparkling deliciousness in pails from whichever spring was nearest their home.

My father was so afraid of fire that he dug many wells on his land and had also two great cisterns for soft water. Everyone had a rain barrel or two at the corners of his house. The well under our kitchen was deep and had a spring at the bottom. Two pumps stood side by side in our kitchen. One was for well water and one was a cistern pump —water from the former was hard and clear, from the cistern it was brownish and soft.

When Beaver Lake water was piped into Victoria, everyone had taps put in their kitchen and it was a great event. House walls burst into lean-to additions with vent pipes piercing their roofs. These were new bathrooms. With the coming of the water system came sewerage. The wretched little "privies" in every backyard folded their evil wings and flapped away—Victoria had at last outgrown them and was going stylish and modern.

Father built a beautiful bathroom. Two sides of it were of glass. It was built over the verandah and he trained his grape-vine round the windows. The perfume of the vine in spring poured through the open windows deliciously.

Father had tried to build several bathrooms before Beaver Lake came to town, but none of them had been any good. First he used a small north room and had a cistern put in the attic to fill the bathtub. But hot water had to be lugged upstairs in a bucket and anyway the cistern froze every winter; so that bathroom was a failure. He had made us an enormous, movable wooden tub like a baby's bath big enough for a grown-up to lie in flat. It was very heavy and lived on the back verandah. Bong brought it into the kitchen on Saturday nights before he left for town. It had to be filled and emptied over and over by the ladies of the household with a long-handled dipper until all the family had had their baths. Besides this Saturday night monster there were wooden wash tubs painted white which lived under our beds. We pulled these out at night and filled them with cold water. Into this we were supposed to plunge every morning. This was believed to harden us; if your nose were not blue enough at the breakfast table to guarantee that you had plunged, there was trouble.

Father later tried a bathroom off the wash-house across the yard. A long tin pipe hung under the chin of the wash-house pump and carried cold water, but hot water had to be dipped out of the wash boiler on the stove. This hot bath arrangement was bad; we got cold crossing the yard afterwards. So the wooden tub was invited into the kitchen again each Saturday night until we became "plumbed".

It was glorious having Beaver Lake pour out of taps in your kitchen and we gloated at being plumbed. Mothers were relieved to see wells filled in, to be rid of the constant anxiety of their children falling in and being well-drowned. Everyone was proud and happy about this plumbing until the first hard frost.

Victoria used to have very cold winters. There was always some skating and some sleighing and spells of three or four days at a time when the wind from the north would pierce everything. Mother's milk pans in the dairy froze solid. We chopped ice-cream off the top to eat with our morning porridge. Meat froze, bread froze, everything in the house froze although the big hall stove was red hot and there were three or four roaring grate fires as well. Windows were frosted in beautiful patterns all day and our breath smoked.

It was then discovered that plumbers, over-driven by the rush of modern arrangements, had neglected to protect the pipes from frost. Most of the bathrooms were built on the north side of the houses and everything froze except our deep kitchen well. Neighbours rushed to the Carr pump, spilling new snow over Mother's kitchen floor till our house was one great puddle and the kitchen was filled with the icy north wind. Everyone suddenly grumbled at modern plumbing. When the thaw came and all the pipes burst everyone wished Beaver Lake could be piped right back to where it came from.

Once Victoria had started modern off she flew with all sorts of newfangled notions. Cows were no longer allowed to roam the streets nor browse beside open ditches. The ditches were replaced by covered drains and, if your cow wandered into the street, she was impounded and you had to pay to get her out. Dogs were taxed but were still allowed to walk in the streets. A pig you might not keep within so many yards of your neighbour's nose. Jim Phillips had to give up his James' Bay farm and remove his piggery to the country. Small farms like his were wanted for cutting into city lots. You never knew when new lumber might be dumped on any piece of land and presently the lumber was a house and someone was moving in.

Jim Phillips' big turnip field across from us was made into the Caledonian Park, a place for the playing of public ball and lacrosse games. It was fenced high and close and admission was charged. The gate of Caledonian Park was on the corner of Simcoe and Carr Streets, just opposite us. There was a long, unpainted building inside, which was the players' dressing room. Bob Foster lived there. He was the boys' trainer and one of those ousted-out-of-England ne'er-do-wells. There was some good in old Bob but drinking spoiled it. He trained, rubbed down and doctored the boys for sprains and hurts on the field. He took good care of the boys and the boys took care of Bob. He owned a little white dog whom he also trained to scour the neighbourhood for somebody else's hen and bring her home for Bob's dinner parties. The noise of these parties flew over our hedge, filled our garden all night and made our dreams bad.

Caledonian Park existed for many years but finally the lease expired and then the land was cut into building lots.

Just before the high board fence came down a Barnum and Bailey Circus (three rings and a menagerie) came to town. It came at night, so silently that we slept through its arrival. Before it was fully light little boys had their eyes glued to knot holes in the board fence. Tops of great tents poked tantalizingly into the sky.

The Circus gave free passes to boys who lugged water for the animals. When every beast was full, even the elephants and the seven stomachs of the camel, a little boy came; he was too late to get any job. He was feeling very sad when a tall, lean man popped out of a tent.

"Say, son, I gotta have a dress shirt in an hour. Hand over one of your pa's and you git a pass."

As the little boy started to run home, the man shouted, "Yer pa's fat? Then bring along safety pins!"

The boy and his mother argued a bit about Pa's shirt, but the boy not only got into the big tent free, he could boast of having pinned a real live clown into his father's shirt—more exciting even than watering an elephant.

From Carr Street to James' Bay

WHEN FATHER started for town in the morning I went with him down the drive to the gate, holding his hand. The gate stood between two high, high Lombardy poplars. Their tops were right up in the sky. If you could have got to their tippy tops you could have spoken right into God's ear.

Father planted our poplars when they were little. The two by the gate were the tallest.

The bigger I grew the farther I was allowed to go with Father. When I was seven I went as far as the Lindsays'.

We got up early in our house. I came downstairs perfectly clean but when it was time for Father to go to town I was dirty because of being such great friends with the hens and ducks. And then I always sat by Carlow for a little because he was chained to his kennel. His feet and chain made lots of dust on me and the leaks from the can when I watered my own particular garden made it into mud.

As soon as Father began to go he went quickly, so Mother made me a "jump-on-top" of sprigged muslin. It went over my head so that there were no buttons to burst off. There were frills all round it and a tape tieback underneath. The front sat plain but the back bunched up into a bustle like a lady's. I had a pair of cloth-top, button boots and a sun-bonnet. I looked quite nice when I took Father's hand and we started.

Father walked fast and held my hand tight. The plank walk was just wide enough for us both but, if you did not watch, your foot slipped off into the mud. We did not talk much because Father was thinking of all the things he had to do at his big wholesale business where boxes and barrels and cases stood on top and on top and on top, till they touched the ceiling. When he thought hard a ditch came between Father's eyebrows; then I did not dare to chatter. I just looked at things as we went along. It was on the way home that I got to know "the ladies".

Our street was called Carr Street after my Father. We had a very nice house and a lovely garden.

Opposite our gate was Bishop Cridge's "wild field". It was full of trees and bushes and fallen logs and was a grand place to play ladies with little girls. The Bishop's house and garden were beyond the field. The drive was curved and had laurels and roses down it so you could not see his house. Then came his big field with the barn in the corner where his horse and cow lived. The field was so big it took up all the rest of Carr Street. There was a well in it where the Cridges got their water to wash and drink. Every morning we saw the Chinaman carrying two square coal oil cans of water across the field, they dangled one on each end of a pole and slopped a little over the stubble.

On the other side of Carr Street where our poplars ended the Fawcetts' place began. They had hundreds of heavy, wide children with curls. Their clothes were always too big. Their mother told our mother that she made them that way because she knew her children would grow. Mrs. Fawcett was wide too and had very crimpy hair and a crooked neck; "Pa" Fawcett was tremendously lean and tall and had a long, thin beard.

Then came the Bishop's field—not Bishop Cridge's but Bishop Hill's. He did not live in his field; there were cows there. One corner had a thicket with wild lilies growing in it. The two Bishops did not like each other much and it was a good thing there were two fences between their cows. There were picket fences all the way down Carr Street. The fences stopped suddenly because Mrs. McConnell's farm sat right in the way and had a rail fence of its own.

Carr Street was a very fine street. The dirt road waved

up and down and in and out. The horses made it that way, zigzagging the carts and carriages through it. The rest of the street was green grass and wild roses. There was a grand, wide open ditch with high grass by the sides. The cows licked in great mouthfuls to chew as they walked up and down to the pasture land at the end of Carr Street down by the beach. In front of our place Father had made a gravel walk but after our trees stopped there were just two planks to walk on.

At Mrs. McConnell's farm Father and I turned into Toronto Street. It was not half so fine; there was only a one-plank walk so we had to go one in front of the other. The ditch was little and mean, too. When we came to "Marifield Cottage" we turned into Princess Avenue. It was smaller still and had no ditch and no sidewalk. It was just a green strip pinched in between two fences. If two carts came in at both its ends at the same time one of them had to back out.

Uncle Jack's garden was on one side of Princess Avenue. He was not uncle to everybody but everybody called him that. He was a kind man who did jobs. When he worked for Father he took us for rides in his cart. It had no seat— just a loose plank laid across the cart. If the plank slid, Uncle Jack held on to you. There was such a high fence round his place that nothing could look over except the lilacs and the may trees. Their smell tumbled right over the fence on to you.

Opposite Uncle Jack's was Mrs. Swannick's house. She had no nose, only a wrinkle and two holes. She had a sick son, too. Before he died Father sent him a bottle of brandy because he was so very sick. Mrs. Swannick was so glad she cried. Her hands went up and she said, "O Lor! It's 'three star', too!"

Mrs. Robinson's house came next. She was a stout lady. She had a great friend named Mrs. Johnson who lived up past our house. Mrs. Robinson went every day to see Mrs.

Johnson and Mrs. Johnson walked home with Mrs Robinson; then Mrs. Robinson walked back with Mrs. Johnson. They went up and down, up and down; at last they stopped at our gate which was just about half way and then each ran home alone. These ladies were very fond of each other.

The last house on Princess Avenue was Mrs. Lipsett's. She was skinny and red, her nose and chin and elbows were sharp. She was always brushing or shaking something but no dirt ever came out. Her skinny arms hugged the great mattresses and plumped them onto her window ledges, as far as they could go without falling out, so that they could be sunned. It made Mrs. Jack very angry to see Mrs. Lipsett's beds hanging out of the windows. That is why "Uncle" put up such a high fence. It went all round the corner onto Michigan Street and shut out everything else as well as the beds and made it dark for poor Mrs. Jack—like living behind the world. Mrs. McConnell's front came right next to Uncle Jack's fence.

Mrs. McConnell was a splendid lady; I liked her very much indeed. She had such a large voice you could hear it on Toronto Street, Princess Avenue and Michigan Street all at once. She was so busy with all her children and cows and pigs and geese and hens that she had no time to be running after things, so she stood in the middle of her place and shouted and everything came running—Joseph, Tommy, Lizzie, Martha-Anne, Spot, Brownie and Daisie, and when she yelled "Chuck, Chuck, Chuckie" the whole farm was wild with wings. Something was always running to Mrs. McConnell. She sort of spread herself over the top of everything about the place and took care of it.

Mrs. McConnell worked very hard. She sold milk and eggs and butter and pork. She let people go through her place instead of round by Princess Avenue if they wanted to. Father did not, but I often used to come home that way because I liked Mrs. McConnell and her things. She called me "Lovey" and showed me her calves and little pigs. She said I was a "faithful lamb" taking my "Pa" to town every morning, but really it was Father who took *me*. She was Irish, with shiny eyes and high red cheeks, black hair and long teeth with wide gaps where there were not any; when she laughed you saw the gaps. The windows of Mrs. McConnell's and Mrs. Cameron's houses peered down Birdcage Walk like a pair of spectacles.

I don't remember what was on the corner of Birdcage Walk opposite Mrs. Cameron's "spectacle". Mrs. Cameron had a lot of cows, too, and a big barn with a little windmill on the top. All the wind running down Birdcage Walk caught it and turned the wheel. Mrs. Cameron had quite white hair, bundled into a brown net. She had a pink face with a hole of a mouth that had no teeth in it, only a pink tongue which rolled round when she talked, and a fluffy chin. She was a dear old lady and had two daughters. Jessie was the oldest and had a turned-up nose; her mouth turned up too when she laughed, and when she met her friends she began to bow by jerking her head away back on her neck and then she bounced it forward like a sneeze. Agnes was very clever: she taught school and quarrelled with the trustees. She wrote things that were printed too.

Mrs. McConnell's "spectacles" looked right across at Mrs. Plummer who was on the corner of Michigan and Birdcage Walk. Mrs. Plummer lived in a field—that is, her house sat in the middle of a very big field. Her cottage was made of corrugated iron and had a verandah all round it. The most splendid thing about it was that every window was a door made of glass and coming to the floor, so that Mrs. Plummer could rush straight out of any room into her garden—like a swallow darting out of a bank—she did not have to go through passages first. I expect that is why she built her house just like that, with so many doors. Her garden had a little fence round it to keep the cows in the big field from eating her flowers. Because of there being two fences round Mrs. Plummer I did not get to know her,

157

but I saw her sometimes. She had a reddish face and a purple dress and was thick round the middle. In my own mind I called her "Mrs. Plum". When a cow looked over her fence she burst out of one of the "door windows" shouting "Shoo-shoo-shoo!" and beat one of her mats to show the cow what she meant. I always hoped Mrs. Plummer would come rushing out as we passed.

Birdcage Walk was almost a very grand street because the Parliament Buildings were nearly on it. Just a little row of houses was between. Besides, if it had not been for James' Bay Ridge breaking in, Birdcage Walk would have been Government Street which was the most important street in Victoria. Birdcage Walk was wide and had a plank walk on both sides—wide enough to pass other people as you walked on it and it had a covered-in drain, too.

The Wilsons lived in the big house on the corner after Mrs. Plummer. They had a large family and a beautiful pine tree that was not a pine at all . . . it came from another country. The lawn where the children played was down three steps from the flower garden. Mr. Wilson was square and looked pressed hard as if he had grown up under something heavy. Mrs. Wilson was like a bird, with a sharp little nose. She wore her hair cut in a tiny fringe where the parting ended.

Then came the birdcagy part of Birdcage Walk—some funny little square houses with a chimney right in the middle of the top of each like a handle to hang it up by. In the first of these little houses Miss Wylie lived. She was squeaky and quite old. Her brother Charlie lived with her. He was very, very deaf. Miss Wylie had to squeak very high indeed for Charlie to hear her at all. Generally he said "Yes—yes —ah, yes—Tillie," but did not hear a word. Miss Wylie was a very timid lady. When she was coming to see Mother she sent word first so that Mother could send me down to fetch her, because she was so afraid of meeting a cow. I did feel brave walking up Carr Street on the ditch side of Miss Wylie, sucking one of her peppermints, particularly if there was a cow down in the ditch and I could look over the top of her back and horns.

Mrs. Green in the "birdcage" opposite the Wylie's was very kind to the Wylies because they were old. The Greens were important people: Mr. Green was a banker. They had a lot of children so they had to build more and more pieces on to their house till it did not look like a birdcage any more. The Greens had everything—a rocking-horse, real hair on their dolls, and doll buggies, a summerhouse and a croquet set. They gave a Christmas-tree party every year and everyone got a present. The Mason's fence was at the end of the Green's lawn; it was covered with ivy which was a bother for the Green's croquet balls. The Masons had a grey house and a boy, Harry, who was rough and cruel to our dolls.

And now we had come to the Lindsays and James' Bay Bridge was just in front. Then Father doubled down and kissed me goodbye. Across the Bridge there was a saloon on every corner, so I was not allowed to go any farther. I waved to Father on the Bridge and then I was free.

I peeped between the stalky parts of the Lindsays' lilacs. Their gate had an arbour and you went down two steps into the garden. Next to Mrs. Plummer's I liked the Lindsays' place the best. There was a round flowerbed in the middle of their garden with a little path round it. All the rest of the garden was bushes and shrubs. Everything sweet grew in the Lindsays' garden. Perhaps they did it because sometimes the mud flats under James' Bay Bridge smelt awful. There was mignonette and cabbage roses and little yellow roses and red ones and moss ones. You could hardly see the house for vines, honeysuckle and clematis—then there were the lilacs, much purpler and sweeter than anyone else's.

As I went on home everyone nodded to me, but Miss Jessie Cameron gave me a whole bow as if I were a grown-up lady.

I often took the short cut through Mrs. McConnell's farm.

She never stopped flying round but she always said, "Well, Lovey, is it yourself sure?" I always shut her gates most carefully.

One morning Mother gave me a beautiful bunch of flowers. She said I was only to go with Father as far as Mrs. McConnell's front gate and then I was to take the flowers to Mrs. McConnell and say they were for the baby.

I tapped at the door . . . everything was quite still. Instead of shouting, "Come right in", Mrs. McConnell came and opened the door quietly. Her eyes were red.

"Mother sent some flowers for your baby, Mrs. McConnell."

"Come and give them to him, Lovey."

She took my hand and led me in. I looked round, expecting to see the baby sitting in his pram. I was going to bounce the flowers at him and hear him giggle. The pram was not there. There was a little table in the middle of the room with a white box on it. Mrs. McConnell put her hands under my arms and lifted me so that I could look into the box. The baby was there—asleep, but his eyes were not quite shut.

Mrs. McConnell said, "Kiss him, Lovey". I kissed the baby's cheek. It was hard and cold. I dropped the flowers on his feet. Mrs. Cameron came in then, so I slipped out and ran home.

"Mother, why was Mrs. McConnell's baby so cold and funny?"

"Did you see the baby?"

"I kissed him. Mrs. McConnell told me to."

Mother looked vexed. She told me about death but I only half understood. I did not take the short cut for a long time after that but went round by Mrs. Lipsett's and Mrs. Swannick's.

The worst thing about Carr Street was that the houses were set far back in the gardens. There was nothing to see except what was in the street. Often the Bishop's chaise was going in or out and I ran to open the gate for Mrs.

Cridge. It was a very big, low, wide chaise. There was a high hook for the reins to hang over so that they could not get swished under old Charlie's tail. He was a very lazy old horse and never ran. You could get in and out of the chaise while Charlie was going. They never stopped him because it was so hard to start him again. When Mrs. Cridge got very impatient to get anywhere she stood up and flapped the reins on Charlie's back. Then Charlie lashed his tail across the reins and pinned them down so tight that Mrs. Cridge could not drive at all and had to hang over the front and work at them. Her face went red and her bonnet crooked but all she ever said was "Ahem!" and "Oh, Charlie! Charlie!" The Bishop sat beside her smiling, with his eyes shut. Charlie held the reins down tight and pretended Mrs. Cridge was stopping him. Then by and by, when she had fished his tail up off the reins with the whip handle, he went on.

Every morning I ment the Johnson girl on Carr Street. The Johnsons had a vegetable garden round the corner and their girl carried the vegetables to people in a basket. I don't know what her name was. We never spoke. She was taller than I and had a flat body and a meek face . . . which made me angry. After she had passed I always turned round and made a face at her. She knew I was going to so she looked back. One morning she had a big basket of potatoes on her arm and I made a dreadful face. She looked so hard and long that she tripped and sprawled in the mud, all her potatoes flying into the ditch. I laughed right out loud and stood watching while she fished them out. Her apron was all mud. She took it off and wiped each potato and put it back onto the basket. She did not look at me or say one word. When the potatoes were wiped and back in the basket she wiped first one of her eyes and then the other on the muddy apron, picked up her basket and went on down the street.

I went home too. I felt the meanest, meanest meanest thing I had ever heard of. Why didn't the Johnson girl hit me? Or throw mud, or say something? Why didn't she?

Father and Mother were talking about it . . . I was old enough but I cried every time I thought about going to school. My sisters tramped two miles night and morning. If I went with them I would not be able to see Mrs. Lipsett's bed or Mrs. Swannick's nose or Mrs. Plummer fly out or Miss Jessie's bow. We'd go on a straight, horrible road that had no friends on it . . . but, I did not have to.

Mrs. Fraser, the lady who had come to live in "Marifield Cottage" started a little school, so I went there. I could still go as far as the gate of the school every morning with Father, and on Saturdays I could go right to the Lindsays and see all my friends.

When Saturday came I wanted to tell Father something, only it wouldn't come out. I looked up a lot of times but the ditch between his eyes was very deep—I was half afraid. We had passed the Greens' . . . we were at the Masons' steps . . . the Lindsays' lilacs were just coming.

"Father—Father—don't you think—now that I go to school I am too big to be kissed in the street?"

"Who said so?"

"The girls at school."

"As long as I have to stoop you won't be too big," Father said, and he kissed me twice.

Grown Up

VICTORIA's top grandness was the Driard Hotel; all important visitors stayed at the Driard. To sit in crimson plush armchairs in enormous front windows and gaze rigid and blank at the dull walls of the opposite side of View Street so close to the Driard Hotel that they squinted the gazer's eyes, to be stared at by Victoria's inhabitants as they squeezed up and down narrow View Street which had no view at all, was surely worth a visit to the capital city.

The Driard was a brick building with big doors that swung and squeaked. It was red inside and out. It had soft red carpets, sofas and chairs upholstered in red plush and rep curtains, red also. All its red softness sopped up and hugged noises and smells. Its whole inside was a jumble of stuffiness which pushed itself into your face as you opened the outer door, licking the outside freshness off you greedily, making a dash for the open. But the Driard door squawked and slammed to before the stuffiness could escape and hit back smotheringly onto you. When you came out of the hotel you were so soaked with its heaviness you might have been a Driard sofa. Even the hotel bus had the Driard odor, although it did not actually live inside the hotel. It was a long, jolty two-horse bus with "Driard" painted on both its sides and a man shouting "Driard" from the back step. Stow-away Driard smells hid in the cushions of the bus and drove to the wharf ready to pounce on visitors.

The Driard visitors came mostly from San Francisco; Vancouver and Sound cities were too busy growing to waste time on visiting.

Victoria and Vancouver were always rivals and made jealous faces at one another. Vancouver had a finer harbour and grew faster; she was the easier to reach, being the end of the rail. Victoria had the Queen's name, was the capital of British Columbia and had the Esquimalt Naval Station.

When the East and West were linked by the Canadian Pacific Railway, Vancouver said, "Ha! I am the end of the rail; nobody will now bother about that little Victoria town on her island. Settlers and visitors will get off the train and stay here with me."

So she built factories, lumber mills, wharves and swelled herself furiously; but no matter how she swelled she could not help Victoria's being the capital of British Columbia or having the Naval Station. The navy men's wives came from England direct to Victoria to live while their husbands' ships were stationed at Esquimalt a mile or so out of the city.

Victoria kept in closer touch with England. She got more and more "Old Country"; Vancouver got more and more new-world. Vancouver coveted Victoria's gentility; Victoria coveted Vancouver's business.

These two cities made Canada's West, her far Pacific edge which lured pioneers on and on till they came to the rim of the ocean, earth bent to the world's roundness—land and water circling the West back to the East again.

Pioneers slid across Canada's vastness on the C.P.R. trains and were so comfortable in doing it that they did not get off till they had to. Often the first Canadian land their feet touched was British Columbia. The stark West snarled a little when they touched her first but she was really nearer to England in her ways and feelings than the East was, although the West was some four thousand miles farther away in space. By and by the English forgave the West her uncouth vastness and the West forgave them their narrow littleness.

The C.P.R. watched the West grow. She saw Victoria's squatty little old red brick Parliament Buildings give place to magnificent stone structures—domes, copper roofs—everything befitting a Capital City. Facing the Parliament

Buildings across James' Bay arose a sedate stone and cement
Post Office. Little old knock-kneed wooden James' Bay
bridge still straddled the mud flats between the two. The
C.P.R. pillowed their heads upon the mud flats and dreamed
a dream. First they tore down the old wooden bridge and
built in its place a wide concrete causeway, damming the
Bay waters back from the flats. The sea was furious and
dashed, but the concrete wall hurled it back. Smells got
frantic and stank to high Heaven until engineers came and
drained the seepage slough.

Pendray's soap works and Kanaka Row could not endure
life without smells,—so they just faded out of existence.
The soap-fat refuse from the soap works stopped playing
glorious iridescent colours across the mud when the sun
shone. No tide came in to sweep away Kanaka Row's
refuse: their back doors were heaped round with it and
were disgusting. The yellow clay of the mud flats parched
and cracked. The mash grass, through which the Indian
canoes had slithered so caressingly, turned harsh and brittle.

The City bartered with the Songhees Indians giving them
money and a new reserve at Esquimalt in exchange for their
fine harbour properties, which the City wanted for indus-
trial purposes. All around Victoria's little harbour there was
change. Even our dumpy little concept of Queen Victoria,
drawn from the *Illustrated London News* changed when
a swarthy stone amazon rose on a pedestal in front of the
Parliament Buildings. Except for the crown and sceptre
we would never have recognized this as our civic godmother.

While these changes were wrecking Victoria's calm, the
C.P.R. were still dreaming their mud-flat dream and archi-
tects were making blue prints of it. To be private and un-
disturbed during their dreaming they built a huge hoarding
the entire length of the causeway shutting the dream into
the mud. A citizen's eye was applied to every knot-hole
in the hoarding but they could make neither head nor tail
of what was going on. The pile-driver gawked over the top
of the hoarding. Thud, thud, thud! Her fearful weight

obeyed the squeaky little whistle of her engine, driving mighty logs, each one a complete tree-bole, end down into the mud. There they stood shoulder to shoulder, a headless wooden army tramping the old mud-smells clean through to China. When the flats were a solid wooden pack the harbour bottom was dredged and the liquid mud pumped in between the standing logs. Thousands of men wheeled millions of barrowloads of earth and rocks for hundreds of weeks—dumping, loading till solid ground was made on which the C.P.R. could found their dream.

The dream took shape in reality. The hoarding came down at last and there stood the beautiful Empress Hotel. It never looked crude and new because, while the back was building, the finished front was already given over to creepers and shrubs, and gardens were set the moment workmen's feet had stopped trampling. Beautiful conservatories sat right on top of where the city garbage dump had once been. Under their glass roofs bloomed rare flowers from all parts of the world, but none were more sweet, more lovely than the little wild briar roses that had so graciously soothed our noses over the old mud-flat smells.

The Driard Hotel could not blush herself any redder than she already was when confronted by her rival so she withered entirely away. No visitors wanted to sit enthroned on red plush, to stare at brick two feet from their noses when they could sit behind plate glass and look out over Victoria's lovely little harbour. Beautiful steamers snuggled up to the wharf, almost to the very door of the Hotel. From London dock to Empress Hotel door was one uninterrupted slither of easy travel.

Victoria ceased to be an English naval station: Canada navied herself. Esquimalt Harbour now had a huge dry-dock and a cannery. A few Indian dug-out canoes stole in and out to the new reservation but most of the Indians now came and went in their new gas fishing-boats.

Victoria knew a little boom—a little bustle—but it was not her nature to boom and bustle; she slumped, settling to slow easy development—reticent, calm, deliberate.

These enormous happenings—the building of the Parliament Buildings, Empress Hotel and Causeway, the establishing of a first class boat service between the Island and the mainland stirred the heart of Victoria and sent lesser happenings quivering through her outskirts.

The narrow, three-mile strip of warm, inland sea opening out of the harbour and called the Gorge because of a narrow pass half-way up its course, one of Victoria's beauty spots where her people had bathed, and where regattas had been held on the Queen's birthday, became infested with booms of logs and saw-mills. Bathers protested. They did not like sawdust skins after bathing in the Gorge waters so went to the swimming tanks in the Y.M.C.A. and in the Crystal Pool of the new Empress Hotel. The Gorge that had once been so fine a residential district went unfashionable. The beautiful homes on its banks sold for a mere song. Canoes and row-boats ceased carrying pleasure parties up its protected waters to picnic. The fleet of sailing schooners still stuck to their winter quarters just below the Point Ellice bridge, where the harbour ended and the Gorge began, coming back to its safeness every winter like homing birds. A hideous railway bridge now spanned the Harbour and carried trains from "up-island" into the city. Spanning the upper harbour this bridge hoisted a section of itself for the sealers to pass under and then shut them safe in shelter.

Cedar Hill lying to the north of the town went "snooty"; elevating her name to Mount Douglas, she became a Public Park, smug with tameness. Little Saanich Mountain hatted her crown with an observatory the white dome of which looked for all the world like an inverted white pudding basin.

Because there was no more English Navy stationed at Esquimalt there were no more navy balls and no sham battles between the soldiers and sailors on Beacon Hill. There were no more road-house saloons with lovely flower boxes and cages of wild animals and horses' drinking troughs —there were no more driving horses. Automobiles purred over oiled and paved highways and there was no dust to make people and horses thirsty.

From the top of Church Hill the Cathedral stepped one block back. Instead of dominating the city she now dominated the old Quadra Street cemetery long since replaced by the new Ross Bay burying ground. Brambles no longer overran the dead Pioneers. Victoria's early settlers slept tidily under well mown lawns. The old head-stones and name-boards had been huddled into a corner, glowering morosely from their pale names, resenting the nakedness of being without the clinging vines and the riot of undergrowth that had protected their dead and themselves. On benches the public sat on top of the dead. Children scampered over them—jangle of the new cathedral bells quivered the dead's stillness.

James' Bay is James' Bay still. The smart forsook her long ago. First they moved to Upper Fort Street, then to Rockland Avenue, then on to Oak Bay, finally to the Uplands where they could not keep a cow or hang out a wash or have too many children. The entire shore line of greater Victoria is now spread with beautiful homes.

Victoria's inner land being higher than her shore, every aspect is lovely, North, South, East and West—blue sea, purple hills, snow-capped Olympic mountains bounding her southern horizon, little bays and beaches heaped with storm-tossed drift, pine trees everywhere, oak and maple in plenty.

So stands tranquil Victoria in her Island setting—Western as West can be before earth's gentle rounding pulls West east again.

Books in the Clarke Irwin Canadian Paperback series: